"Among the many myths of modernity, none has been more devastating to the church than the belief that method is what matters most in ministry. And nowhere has this myth been more pernicious than in preaching. Steeped in homiletical method, preaching is now more rhetorically sophisticated and entertaining than ever, but the life-changing power of the gospel is conspicuous by its absence. Fortunately, in *Give Them Christ,* the help that we so desperately need has arrived. Indeed, for all those who long to recover the transforming power of preaching, I can think of no better place to begin."

JASON E. VICKERS, professor, United Theological Seminary

"If you want an antidote to the marketed Jesus of popular evangelical imagination and a return to the faithful Christology of the New Testament, then you have found it in Steve Seamands's *Give Them Christ.* Seamands brings the reader on a very engaging, accessible journey that introduces us afresh to the awesome truth of the incarnation, the costly scandal of the cross, the glorious magnificence of the resurrection and the triumphant glory of the ascension. The result is a Christology for the church that will surprise and delight Christians everywhere. I heartily recommend it!"

TIMOTHY C. TENNENT, president, Asbury Theological Seminary

"Preaching is Christology in thoughtful, contextually connected and passionate speech. Stephen Seamands knows this. The gospel has no other content than Jesus Christ, and that means his incarnation, crucifixion, resurrection, ascension and return. In *Give Them Christ* Seamands artfully presents us with the sifted wisdom of his gleanings from exegesis, theology, hymnody, poetry, biography and even cultural analysis. This book on what to preach—and not on how to preach—has the order right, for form follows content. Clearly written, with never a point without illustration, this is a book that will gladden the preacher for the work of warming the hearts, stirring the imaginations and renewing the minds of the people with the gospel of Jesus Christ."

ANDREW PURVES, professor of Reformed theology, Pittsburgh Theological Seminary, author of *The Crucifixion of Ministry*

"As a preacher and a teacher of preachers I am profoundly encouraged by *Give Them Christ*. Seamands has called the pulpit to meet the needs of a generation largely without knowledge of Christian doctrine. Concentrating on the doctrines related to the person of Christ, he demonstrates not only the importance of doctrine but also how exciting and winsome such preaching can be. He offers sound scholarship delivered with passion."

J. ELLSWORTH KALAS, professor of homiletics, Asbury Theological Seminary

"Nothing is more important than for pastors to lift up Christ in their preaching. Here is a book designed to help them do exactly that—in a way that will help their congregations understand the significance of what Christ has done for their personal lives and their life together."

JIM GARLOW, senior pastor, Skyline Wesleyan Church

"With this book, Steve Seamands calls pastors and congregations to remember that Jesus Christ is the heart of the gospel, and not just a means we use to carry out and advance the mission of the gospel. Guided by his love for both theology and the church, Seamands challenges the contemporary trend to offer "Christianity without Christ" and offers instead a well-argued and clearly articulated presentation of the gospel as it is manifested in the whole witness of Scripture. Seamands thus helps us to see how preaching and theology continue to need each other if the church is to be faithful to its calling. This timely work will provide wisdom and encouragement to all who long to see a renewal of preaching in our time."

MICHAEL PASQUARELLO III, Granger E. and Anna A. Fisher Professor of Preaching, Asbury Theological Seminary

STEPHEN SEAMANDS

GIVE

PREACHING HIS INCARNATION,

THEM

CRUCIFIXION, RESURRECTION,

CHRIST

ASCENSION AND RETURN

IVP Books

An imprint of InterVarsity Press
Downers Grove, Illinois

InterVarsity Press
P.O. Box 1400, Downers Grove, IL 60515-1426
World Wide Web: www.ivpress.com
E-mail: email@ivpress.com

InterVarsity Press® is the book-publishing division of InterVarsity Christian Fellowship/USA®, a movement of students and faculty active on campus at hundreds of universities, colleges and schools of nursing in the United States of America, and a member movement of the International Fellowship of Evangelical Students. For information about local and regional activities, write Public Relations Dept., InterVarsity Christian Fellowship/USA, 6400 Schroeder Rd., P.O. Box 7895, Madison, WI 53707-7895, or visit the IVCF website at <www.intervarsity.org>.

Unless otherwise indicated, all Scripture quotations are taken from the Holy Bible, New Living Translation, copyright ©1996. Used by permission of Tyndale House Publishers, Inc., Wheaton, Illinois 60189. All rights reserved.

While all stories in this book are true, some names and identifying information in this book have been changed to protect the privacy of the individuals involved.

Lyrics for "Christ Is Risen" by Matt Maher and Mia Fieldes: Copyright © 2009 Shout! Publishing (ASCAP) (adm. in the US and Canada at EMICMGPublishing.com)/ Thankyou Music (PRS) (adm. worldwide at EMICMGPublishing.com excluding Europe which is adm. by Kingswaysongs) Spiritandsong.Com Pub (BMI) (adm. at EMICMGPublishing.com) International Copyright Secured. All rights reserved. Used by permission.

Cover design: Cindy Kiple
Interior design: Beth Hagenberg
Images: © alexkar08/iStockphoto

ISBN 978-0-8308-3467-9

Printed in the United States of America ∞

Library of Congress Cataloging-in-Publication Data

Seamands, Stephen A., 1949-
    Give them Christ: preaching his incarnation, crucifixion
resurrection, ascension, and return/Stephen Seamands.
        p. cm
    Includes bibliographical references.
    ISBN 978-0-8308-3467-9 (pbk.: alk. paper)
    1. Preaching. 2. Jesus Christ. I. Title.
    BV4211.3.S43 2012
    251—dc23

                                                        2012000261

P	18	17	16	15	14	13	12	11	10	9	8	7	6	5	4	3	2	1
Y	27	26	25	24	23	22	21	20	19	18	17	16	15	14	13	12			

To my eight wonderful grandchildren:

Kayla Marie
Andrew David
Daniel Jay
William Joshua
Hannah Jhin
Jackson Mark
Allie Jo
Graham Benjamin

"Grandchildren are the crowning glory of the aged."
Proverbs 17:6

CONTENTS

1

CHRIST ABOVE ALL

Preach Christ, always and everywhere.
He is the whole Gospel.
His person, His offices and work
must be our one great, all-comprehending theme.

CHARLES SPURGEON

I had first seen the movie as a ten-year-old boy in a missionary boarding school in south India. Fifteen years later, as a young pastor, I was watching it again with seven or eight unenthusiastic middle-schoolers who were part of a late-afternoon confirmation and church membership class I was leading. As part of our ever-so-brief overview of church history, we were watching *Martin Luther,* a black-and-white film released in the 1950s that revolved around Luther's break from Rome and climaxed with his famous "Here I Stand" speech.

That afternoon, however, it was something Luther said earlier in the film that made an indelible impression on me. Luther had nailed his ninety-five theses to the door of the Castle church in Wittenberg and had spoken out against unbiblical church practices such as selling indulgences, praying to saints, goint on pilgrimages, using relics and images, and believing in purgatory. As a result, the entire Christian world was in an uproar.

Now he is back in the seclusion of the monastery and is talking to Von Staupitz, his abbot and spiritual advisor, who is being pressured by bishops and other ecclesiastical leaders to bring his maverick monk in line. "You're right about many things," he says to Luther. "There *are* many abuses in the church. We can't allow them to go on unchecked. They have to be corrected.

"But Martin," Von Staupitz continues, "I'm concerned you're going too far in your protest. You not only want to *correct* the abuses, you've said you want to *eliminate* many of these practices altogether."

Luther nods his head in agreement. "That's right, you've heard me correctly. There's no explicit biblical basis for these practices, so they need to be abolished."

Von Staupitz and Luther go back and forth. The abbot is sympathetic with many of his monk's concerns and patiently tries to reason with him. Eventually, however, he realizes it's no use. Luther won't budge and is adamant about his radical approach to reform.

Finally, in exasperation, Von Staupitz exclaims, "But Martin, if we get rid of all these things—the saints, the pilgrimages, the images, the relics and the holy days, what will happen? These are the practices the common people cling to and treasure most. What will we give them in their place?"

Luther is quiet for a moment. Then, looking firmly and intently at his superior, he declares, "Why, Sir, we'll give them Christ. Yes, we'll give them Christ."

Those words gripped me that afternoon and still echo in my mind almost forty years later. In fact, my concern about our failure as pastors and Christian leaders to do just that—give them Christ—has prompted me to write this book.

Restoring Christ's Supremacy
Of course, Christians have never been tempted to openly reject

Christ or dispense with him altogether. "Christianity *is* Christ," as we often say, so how could we ever do that? However, time and again throughout history, as was the case in Luther's day, Christians have been tempted to doubt whether Christ is *enough*, to wonder whether Christ alone is supreme and sufficient for Christian faith and practice. Whenever we succumb to this temptation, other beliefs and practices are always elevated and placed alongside him. Inevitably they take center stage and become more important than Christ himself.

Even within the New Testament period, Christians faced this temptation. In fact, most scholars believe that helping a fledgling church withstand it prompted Paul to write his letter to the Colossians. No one is exactly sure about the false teaching that had infiltrated the Christian community at Colossae. According to scholarly consensus, it was an amalgam, a strange mixture of Jewish legalism and Gnostic Greek philosophy.

Derived from distinctively different worldviews, the two seemed to have little in common. In the end, however, they both arrived at the same place by denying that Christ and Christ alone was supreme and sufficient. In Jewish legalism, he was insufficient for salvation. For in addition to trusting in what he had accomplished through his life, death and resurrection, to be saved one had to be circumcised and adhere to the Jewish law (Col 2:16-23). In Greek Gnosticism, Jesus was viewed as an intermediary in a chain of intermediaries between God and the world. Even though he was the highest intermediary, he was still only one among many so his unique identity with God was undercut. Though we should look to him for knowledge of God, we shouldn't rule out looking to others as well.

In writing to the Colossians, at times Paul directly counters and attacks this false teaching. But his primary strategy throughout his letter is positive, not negative. He simply keeps lifting up Christ, exhorting the Colossians to fix their gaze on him (Col

1:15-20; 2:9-15; 3:1-3). Christ is the very image of God. The fullness of God dwells in him. He's the firstborn of all creation, the
head over all things, and the head of the church. In him are all the
hidden treasures of wisdom and knowledge. Nothing and no one
stands as his rival. No one holds a candle to him. He's in a league
of his own. Why in the world, then, would you even think of looking to anyone or anything else for salvation or knowledge of God?
It's there in Christ alone.

Yet often throughout history, Christians have succumbed to the
Colossian temptation—not to dispense with Christ altogether,
but to add to him or so focus on other things that, in reality, Christ
is no longer deemed supreme and sufficient. Consequently periods of renewal in church history, which have led to social reform
and worldwide Christian expansion, have consistently been
marked by a return to a deep-seated conviction of the supremacy
and sufficiency of Christ. So in the Protestant Reformation, for
example, along with *Scripture alone! Grace alone!* and *Faith alone!*
Luther's words in the movie captured what became a fourth rally-
ing cry: *Christ alone!* In his *Institutes,* John Calvin expresses it
eloquently:

> We see that our whole salvation and all its parts are compre-
> hended in Christ [Acts 4:12]. We should therefore take care
> not to derive the least portion of it from anywhere else. If we
> seek salvation, we are taught by the very name Jesus that it
> is 'of him' [1 Cor 1:30]. . . . If we seek redemption, it lies in
> his passion; if acquittal, in his condemnation; if remission of
> the curse, in his cross [Gal 3:13]; if satisfaction, in his sacri-
> fice; if purification, in his blood; if reconciliation, in his de-
> scent into hell; if mortification of the flesh, in his tomb; if
> newness of life, in his resurrection. . . . In short, since rich
> store of every kind of good abounds in him, let us drink our
> fill from this fountain, and from no other.[1]

Like the Protestant Reformation, the Wesleyan revival, which transformed eighteenth-century England, was also marked by a return to the centrality and sufficiency of Christ. John Wesley's account of his life-changing Aldersgate experience in May 1738 is telling: "I felt my heart strangely warmed. I felt I did trust *in Christ alone for salvation*"[2] (italics mine). Although he had been intently pursuing holiness since 1725, until this point Wesley was trusting not in Christ *alone* for salvation, but in Christ *and* his own good works. Now he fully grasped the sole sufficiency of Christ for salvation.

Albert Outler, the renowned Methodist scholar, who meticulously combed Wesley's *Journal* to determine the focus of his fifty years of evangelistic preaching following Aldersgate, describes what he found: "In a hundred different ways on thousands of different occasions, decade after five decades, his one consistent message was Jesus Christ and him crucified. . . . The burden of his evangelical message was always the same; the references are almost monotonous. He speaks of 'preaching Christ,' of 'offering Christ,' 'proclaiming Christ,' 'declaring Christ,' and so forth."[3]

Outler discovered that 1 Corinthians 1:30—"Christ Jesus, who of God is made unto us wisdom, and righteousness, and sanctification, and redemption" (KJV)—was one of Wesley's favorite preaching texts. He found seventy-two places in his *Journal* where Wesley indicated he had preached on it. Moreover, in 1739, during the first six months of the revival, it was Wesley's favorite text. He preached on it on twelve different occasions.[4] Years later, in 1771, the last words he spoke, as he sent Francis Asbury off to head up the Methodist mission in America, were "Offer them Christ."

Periods of revival and reformation are always marked with a renewed emphasis on the supremacy and sufficiency of Christ. The church turns away from its focus on secondary things and, like the apostle Paul, determines to center its message solely on Jesus Christ and his death on the cross (1 Cor 2:2).

JESUS IN AMERICAN CULTURE

In surveying the current scene in America, at first glance it might appear that the church has been doing an adequate job of "giving them Christ." Compared to post-Christian Europe, for example, where Jesus has almost become a historical curiosity, in the United States, Jesus is everywhere. In Sweden, roughly twice as many people identify themselves as atheists than as active members of the Church of Sweden. In England, more than half the population claims no religious affiliation and more than one in five persons believes that Jesus doesn't exist. In the U.S., on the other hand, more than two out of three persons say they have "made a personal commitment to Jesus Christ," and three-fourths maintain they have "felt his presence."[5]

According to Boston University professor Stephen Prothero, in America the Son of God has become a national icon. He describes this in his book *American Jesus:*

> Jesus is also ubiquitous in American popular culture. On the radio, Mick Jagger and Bono sing about looking for the Buddha but finding Jesus Christ. In movie theaters, Jesus films open every few years, as do Jesus plays and musicals on and off Broadway. Readers also have a voracious appetite for Jesus. The Library of Congress holds more books about Jesus (seventeen thousand or so) than about any other historical figure, roughly twice as many as the runner-up (Shakespeare), and Jesus books there are piling up fast.
>
> Finally, Jesus is a fixture on the American landscape—on highway billboards, bumper stickers, and even tattooed bodies. A hot-air balloon Jesus, complete with a purple robe identifying him as "King of Kings, Lord of Lords," can be seen flying across western states. Not far from Disney World, there is a Jesus theme park called The Holy Land Experience. "Christ of the Ozarks," a seven-story statue of a risen Christ,

lords over Eureka Springs, Arkansas. This statue . . . testifies to the tendency of some Americans to confuse bigness with greatness. Yet it testifies as well to Jesus' cultural reach, which extends from coast to coast and deep into the national psyche.[6]

In *Jesus in America,* Richard Fox, a Yale historian, confirms Prothero's analysis. He describes the Jesus found on the American scene as "Personal Savior, Cultural Hero, National Obsession."[7] Where else but in America would people wear WWJD bracelets and display bumper stickers prompting them to ask, "What would Jesus do?" Or launch anti-SUV environmental awareness campaigns with the slogan "What would Jesus drive?" Or market dieting programs like "What would Jesus eat?" Churches can even purchase "GPS Jesus," a Christ child for outdoor Christmas manger scenes with an embedded satellite tracking system designed to prevent theft. Jesus seems ubiquitous in the U.S., "the nation with the soul of a church," as G. K. Chesterton described it. MSNBC's "Morning Joe" Scarborough sums it up well: "Jesus is back. He's bigger than ever. He's a pop culture superstar."[8]

Yet almost everyone who studies the American religious landscape agrees that although the "American Jesus" may be a mile wide, he is only an inch deep and a far cry from the biblical portrait of the strong Son of God. After a carefully researched, well-documented, 250-page presentation of the wide-ranging images of Jesus embraced by Americans over the past two centuries (enlightened sage, sweet savior, manly redeemer and superstar, to name a few), in the concluding chapter of *American Jesus*, Prothero laments the American cultural captivity of Jesus. No doubt, Jesus has transformed the nation, he observes, but the nation has also transformed him. Time after time, he has been dressed up to suit personal fancies, made palatable to cultural tastes and fashioned to promote national interests.

In *Talladega Nights,* when Ricky Bobby, the fictional NASCAR champion played by Will Ferrell, is challenged by his wife, Carley, about praying to the baby Jesus at mealtime, he snaps back, "I like the *Christmas Jesus* best. And I'm saying grace. When you say grace you can say it to grown-up Jesus, teenage Jesus, bearded Jesus, or whoever you want."[9]

There is, as Prothero observes, a peculiar irony in America's infatuation with Jesus: "In the United States, Jesus is widely hailed as the 'King of Kings.' But it is a strange sort of sovereign who is so slavishly responsive to his subjects. . . . The American Jesus is more a pawn than a king, pushed around in a complex game of cultural (and countercultural) chess, sacrificed here for this cause and there for another."[10]

JESUS IN THE AMERICAN CHURCH

Unfortunately, when we move from the culture at large and step inside the typical American church, the Christ we find is not substantially different. As Stephen Nichols observes in *Jesus Made in America,* even in evangelical churches, "Jesus, like most cultural heroes, is malleable."[11] To be sure, in church we will hear many things about Jesus and the salvation he offers that we may not hear in the popular culture. Nevertheless, Jesus is presented essentially the same way: in terms of what he can do for us. He is the Christ who died for our sins and rose from the dead that we might go to heaven when we die; the Christ who offers us joy and peace, who gives our lives purpose and direction; the Christ who wants to help us with our families and our work. In short, he is the Jesus who wants to do good things for us.

Deeply disturbed by what he has observed, David Bryant, long-time leader in church renewal and national prayer movements, has sounded an alarm concerning a crisis of the supremacy of Christ in the contemporary American church. Bryant distinguishes between the centrality of Christ (his right to be at the center of our personal and congregational worlds) and the supremacy of Christ (his right to take us to the center of his world).[12]

Consider, for example, the difference between the two doors mentioned within a short span of three verses in the book of Revelation. The first is the familiar door of Revelation 3:20. Christ stands and knocks at the door of the church and the door of our hearts. Here is a *closed* door we have to open in order to invite Jesus into our world and our lives.

But then John writes, "After this I looked, and there in heaven a door stood open." Then a voice beckoned him, "Come up here, and I will show you what must take place after this" (Rev 4:1 NRSV). Unlike the first closed door, which we are invited to open, this second door is *already* open but has to be entered. And this time, instead of inviting the Lord Jesus to become a part of *our* world, the world of our personal and communal lives and concerns, he invites us to become a part of *his* world, encompassing all heaven and earth, all peoples and nations, involving his lordship over all creation.

The first door has to do with the centrality of Christ; the second with his supremacy. According to Bryant, a focus on the second is conspicuously lacking in the American church today. Consequently, the Christ we offer is domesticated, marginalized and sanitized to serve our own narrow concerns and interests. He presents a number of "trite Christologies" that haunt the American church: Jesus as our handyman, interior decorator, EMT, personal trainer, pharmacist, along with the one he has observed most in American churches—Jesus as our mascot. Bryant describes him like this:

> We welcome Him among us to cheer us on, to inspire our efforts, to give us confidence about the outcome of the contest. But in the end the "game" is really about us, not about him. We call the plays, organize the team, execute the strategies, pile up the points and achieve the wins. . . . Our cheers may be for Him, but our victories are for us. Rarely does it

cross our minds that the *supremacy* of Christ means that He *is* the game in the final analysis. He coaches the players, calls the strategies, quarterbacks the plays, achieves the touchdowns, wins the game, and gets the "write up" the next day.[13]

Jesus, then, is presented in terms of what he can do for us, not in terms of what we can do for him. He is knocking at the door, wanting to come in so he can meet our personal needs. But rarely do we hear him calling us to serve him, to join him in his mission to all the earth.

Like Bryant, missional church leaders Michael Frost and Alan Hirsch also sound the alarm in *ReJesus,* calling for "vandalizing" our co-opted, domesticated portraits of Jesus so he can be recovered as "Wild Messiah."[14] So do Leonard Sweet and Frank Viola. In their *Jesus Manifesto,* they maintain that the church's major disease today is "JDD: Jesus Deficit Disorder."[15] Countless preachers are infected with it and are "giving dozens of sermons, lectures, and messages relegating Jesus to little more than a footnote or a flourish to some other subject. At best, He gets honorable mention."[16] What is desperately needed is a restoration of his supremacy and sovereignty.

PASTORS WHO HAVE LOST CONFIDENCE

My prayer is that in what follows I can help contribute to that restoration. As a pastoral theologian, I am deeply concerned about the "trite Christologies" prevalent in the American church today and particularly with the way those of us who are pastors and Christian leaders have contributed to the problem. We're not solely responsible for the current crisis in Christology in our churches, but as those particularly set apart to preach and teach in the church, surely the lion's share of the responsibility rests upon us.

So let's be honest. Let's admit that for the past few decades we've been doing a less than adequate job "giving them Christ," especially in our proclamation of the gospel. We may have done many other things well, but, by and large, we have failed to do this most necessary thing.

That is what William Willimon discovered when he became a United Methodist bishop in 2004 and resolved not to appoint any ordained elder as a pastor to a church until he had first heard him or her preach. Having previously taught homiletics in seminary and written several books on preaching, over the next two years, he listened to the sermons of over sixty of his pastors. Willimon found that regardless of their theological persuasion, whether they were a staunch conservative or card-carrying liberal, there was an eerie similarity in their preaching:

> Many of their sermons were lively and engaging and most congregations would hear them gladly on a Sunday morning. Yet with most of them, there was little indication that the content of the sermon or the engine driving the proclamation was the gospel of Jesus Christ. . . .
>
> I was struck by how quickly, how effortlessly, and predictably the preacher disposed of a wild story about Jesus and transformed it into a predictable moralistic diatribe about us. Moving from a text that simply declares what Jesus did, and by implication who Jesus is, it was as if the preacher said, "You don't want to hear about Jesus; you want to hear about you." Thus the sermon was mostly anthropology with just a dash of theology. Moving quickly from the biblical text, the pastor asserted a moralistic list of all the things that we need to do if we (in the absence of a living, acting God) are to take charge of our lives, save ourselves by ourselves and run the world.[17]

Hearing these sermons, Willimon wondered whether we have unwittingly become secular humanists with autosalvation as our goal. Church then becomes the place we come to get charged up to go back to run the world on our own terms, our own way. And the sermon, though it may be engaging, relevant, humorous and lively, actually amounts to nothing more than an insufferably boring and moralistic talk we could have heard at Rotary or some other civic club—at least there they serve you lunch!

Thus whenever our preaching "ceases to be about the truth of God in Jesus Christ," Willimon concludes, it "degenerates into another program of human betterment, the old 'Christ has no hands but our hands' sermonette for basically good people who are making progress."[18] Yet the world itself is already proclaiming that message—"you are your own gods"—far more persuasively than we can, so why bother going to church to hear about it?

WHY WE FAIL TO PREACH CHRIST
Why have we failed our congregations in carrying out this crucial and essential task? Although I can think of a number of reasons, I want to highlight two.

Letting felt needs drive our preaching. The first stems from our lack of nerve rooted in our lack of confidence in the sufficiency and the supremacy of Christ. The truth is we're *afraid* to give them Christ—afraid that if we focus too much on *him* and not on *them,* they'll lose interest and turn away. As Gerald McDermott, professor of religion at Roanoke College in Virginia, observes, "In the last 30 years American pastors have lost their nerve to preach a theology that goes against the grain of American narcissism." So they end up preaching a Christ who is "no more than the Dalai Lama, an admirable kind of guy."[19]

Following the Christian calendar, beginning with the season of Advent prior to Christmas and continuing for approximately the next six months, allows us the privilege of recounting the major "movements" or events in Christ's life: his incarnation, death, resurrection, ascension and return. Even in churches that pride themselves on being nonliturgical and barely follow the Christian calendar, it's almost impossible to escape these movements completely.

Yet how many pastors and leaders, in their preaching and teaching, make use of this time to help their congregations seriously grapple with the meaning of these events? How many help them grasp their significance for their personal and congregational lives? How many make it their concern to simply lift up Christ, to extol the excellence of what he has done, convinced that, in and of itself, *his* story has the power to captivate and transform their hearers?

"But I could never do that," many would contend. "People in my congregation aren't interested in those subjects. They'd be bored if I preached on them. Besides, we're trying to attract unchurched people and be seeker-oriented. I've got to preach about topics that seem relevant to their lives."

And so, because of our fear of not getting a hearing or being accused of preaching sermons that are irrelevant, we shy away from making Christ the vital center of preaching. Because of our lack of confidence in the eternal relevance of the gospel story and its power, when rightly proclaimed, to create its own hearing, we succumb to the temptation of allowing the felt needs of people to become the focal point of preaching. So we preach sermons like "Three Keys to a Happy Marriage," "How to Win over Worry," "Redefining Success on the Job," "Parenting for Dummies," "Making a Living or a Life?" "Starting Your Day off Right," "How to Be Confident in Yourself" or "Becoming a Better You."

To be sure, Christ can help us accomplish these things, but when people's felt needs determine the content of our preaching, we end up proclaiming a Christ who is the means to an end—the fulfillment of our needs—not One who is himself the end. As a result, Christ's own story, as incarnate, crucified, risen, exalted and returning Lord, with its own power to captivate and transform, recedes into the background, and the story of what he can do for us takes center stage.

Does this mean we never take into consideration the felt needs of people? Of course not. Sometimes in order to address people's true needs we must start by addressing their felt needs. And if we fail to take their felt needs seriously, we may never get a chance to meet their deepest needs. There is a time and a place for need-oriented preaching, particularly when it is executed in a truly Christ-centered way.

Currently, however, far too much North American preaching is failing to do that. Instead of revolving around Jesus Christ and him crucified, our preaching revolves around the human condition and how to improve it. Human self-esteem, not Christ, has become the object of faith; the pursuit of happiness, not the pursuit of holiness, has become the goal of the Christian life. Such preaching is essentially anthropocentric—an example of the modernist, liberal approach to theology advocated by Friedrich Schleiermacher, which orthodox and evangelical Christians so strongly eschew. By engaging in it, we fall into the very same error we are anxious to avoid!

Often our felt needs are not our truest or deepest needs. As fallen sinners, we are blind to what they are. The gospel itself must reveal them to us. Have you noticed, for example, how often in his conversations with individuals such as Nicodemus (Jn 3:1-16), the rich young ruler (Mk 10:17-23), the woman at the well (Jn 4:1-42) and Simon the Pharisee (Lk 7:36-50), Jesus doesn't directly respond to their statements or questions? Surprisingly, he shifts the dialogue in a distinctly different direction, not because he is rude or indifferent to the person's concerns, but because he wants to minister to their most profound need.

When we let the perceived needs of people set the agenda for preaching, we will ultimately fail to meet their deepest needs. Instead of focusing on people's needs and then showing how Christ can meet them, we do better to focus on Christ himself—who he is and what he has accomplished. When our hearers are captivated and transformed by Christ and what he has done, when they join him in what he is going, their deepest needs will be met in the process and they will gladly follow hard after him.

Jonathan Edwards, who witnessed this happening to people in eighteenth-century New England during the first Great Awakening, describes it eloquently:

> By the sight of the transcendent glory of Christ, true Christians see him worthy to be followed; and so are powerfully drawn after him; they see him worthy that they should forsake all for him: by the sight of that superlative amiableness, they are thoroughly disposed to be subject to him, and engaged to labor with earnestness and activity in his service, and made willing to go through all difficulties for his sake. And it is the discovery of this divine excellency of Christ that makes them constant to him: for it makes a deep impression upon their minds, that they cannot forget him; and they will follow him whithersoever he goes, and it is in vain for any to endeavor to draw them away from him.[20]

The conviction of the "divine excellency of Christ" needs to burn first in the heart of the preacher and then spread throughout the congregation. Sadly, it is often lacking in the American pulpit today. Having lost confidence in his supremacy and sufficiency, we have failed to communicate that Jesus himself is the pearl of great price. That's why so often the Christ we offer is superficial and anemic.

Not knowing how. The second reason we fail to give them Christ stems from ignorance and neglect. "To be a preacher," declares homiletician Thomas Long, "is to be entrusted with the task of speaking the one word that humanity most urgently and desperately needs to hear, the glad tidings of God's redemption in Jesus Christ."[21] Unfortunately, many pastors simply don't know how to preach that one word well. It wasn't modeled for us in the sermons we heard, and our training didn't teach us how to do it. When we were in Bible school or seminary, many of us had to take theology courses where we were taught Christology, the doctrine of the person and work of Christ, and courses in homiletics where we learned to preach. But we never learned to translate our beliefs about Christ into preaching.

Here is where we who teach in theological seminaries must acknowledge our failure. We have focused on the sorts of biblical, historical, systematic and apologetic questions related to Christology that scholars and academics find interesting, but have often failed to address the most vital concerns of pastors. Faced with the responsibility of preparing weekly sermons, they want to know, "How do we preach it?" Our students, then, may graduate adhering to sound Christological doctrine, but are unable to communicate it in an engaging, compelling way. We have taught them the "what"—Jesus Christ, God's only Son, incarnate, crucified, risen, ascended and coming again—but have failed to communicate the "so what"—the meaning and significance of those events for us, both as individuals and as communities.

When we examine the content of the first Christian sermons preached by Peter and Paul as recorded in Acts, we discover that they clearly center upon Christ and what he has done. Regardless of the Jewish or Gentile background of their audience, whether they were in Jerusalem, Antioch, Athens or Rome, the apostles were adept at proclaiming the story of Jesus (the "what") and then explaining its meaning and implications for their hearers (the "so what"). Unfortunately, many North American pastors today seem unable to do that.

In 1797, William Wilberforce, who worked so tirelessly to get the slave trade abolished in England, complained about the dire state of religion and morals in the land. He lamented the preaching in the churches where "the fatal habit of considering Christian morals as distinct from Christian doctrines has imperceptibly gained strength. . . . Even in the majority of sermons today one can scarcely find a trace of biblical doctrine."[22] The same situation prevails in most churches today.

That's why I've written this book. As a professor of Christian doctrine who regularly teaches courses dealing with the person and work of Christ, but as one who considers himself, first and foremost, a pastoral and practical theologian, my desire is to help pastors and Christian leaders preach Christ faithfully, boldly, winsomely and effectively. In the following chapters, that's what I'll be attempting to do.

WHAT TO PREACH

Although there are many ways I could approach this task, I have chosen to concentrate on the *work* of Christ rather than the *person* of Christ. Of course, the two are inextricably bound together. Who Christ is and what he does can never be separated. In reflecting on the work of Christ, then, I will be assuming the core, ecumenical, consensus beliefs of Nicaea and Chalcedon concerning the person of Christ—that he is truly divine, truly human and truly one. I'm doing this not because I believe that issues related to the person of Christ are unimportant or completely settled, but because I want to stay focused on the preacher's task, which has to do most often with proclaiming the significance of the work of Christ as they lead their congregations each year in reviewing and rehearsing the five major movements in Jesus' life and ministry.

I want to concentrate on these, so I'll devote a chapter to his incarnation, two chapters each to his death and resurrection, a chapter to his ascension, and finally a chapter to his return. In each case, I'll be lifting up primary themes or overarching ideas for preaching related to it. *What* should you preach about Christ—incarnate, crucified, risen, ascended and returning—in a way that helps individuals and congregations grasp the profound relevance and understand the far-reaching implications for their worship, life together and mission in the world? That's the principal question I'll be trying to answer.

Notice I said *what* you should preach. I am a pastoral theologian, not a homiletician, so what follows will be different from what you might expect to find in a typical book about preaching: I won't try to tell you how to go about constructing specific sermons based on the themes or big ideas you should preach about, nor will I offer you sermon titles or outlines, or discuss various styles of preaching (expository, topical, narrative, etc.).

Although for eleven years I served as a local church pastor who had to preach almost every week, for over twenty-five years now I've been teaching doctrine in a theological seminary. Consequently, even though I often preach in local churches, the task of weekly sermon preparation is not one in which I am engaged. Because I have been removed from that task for a long time, I won't be including sample sermons of mine to demonstrate what I am talking about. However, I trust that my discussion of the five major movements in Christ's ministry, the Scriptures cited in relation to them and some of my illustrations will serve as useful raw materials for those engaged in the task.

From our discussion in this chapter of both the cultural and ecclesiastical American Jesus, it should be evident that I am primarily addressing pastors and other Christian leaders in the North American cultural and religious context. Yet as one who often engages in ministry in a global context and who regularly teaches pastors and leaders from Africa, Asia, Europe and Latin America, I believe that "giving them Christ" is a crucial challenge for us all. Though our cultural and religious contexts differ significantly, our primary task is the same. In the words of the hymn, "Christ for the world we sing, the world to Christ we bring."[23] So I pray that what follows might help preachers extol, as Jonathan Edwards said, the "excellency of Christ"—incarnate, crucified, risen, ascended and coming again—not only in New York and Nashville, but also in Buenos Aires and Brazzaville, Manila and Moscow, Cairo and Kinshasa, Singapore and Seoul.

EMBODYING THE MESSAGE OF CHRIST

I also pray that in what follows, pastors and leaders might find *themselves* captivated anew by the beauty of Christ, awestruck by his glory and stunned by the significance of what he has done. In his study of the history of Christian preaching, William Willimon observes that "preaching is always revived and carried forth on a rising theological tide. When the messenger is grasped by a significant message, the messenger will find a way to deliver the message, and if the message is significant, God will bless the messenger's efforts." So he concludes, "There is nothing wrong with contemporary preaching that can't be cured through having something to say about and from God."[24]

I believe Willimon is right. Whenever we've got something to say, something to preach, we'll figure out how to preach it. I pray, then, that in the following chapters, as Christ is lifted up, those of us assigned with the task of preaching might be confronted ourselves with his glorious gospel, captured anew by the astounding message that's ours to proclaim.

And, more than that, may we be transformed by it. For if our preaching is to be fruitful, it is not enough merely to clearly understand and declare what Christ has done. According to the New Testament, we must become so intimately united to Christ himself that we ourselves share in the movements in his life (cf. Rom 6:3-6; Gal 2:20; Eph 2:4-7; Phil 2:5-11; Col 3:1-4). Indeed, we must *embody* the message we proclaim.

In his 1877 Yale Lectures on Preaching, Phillips Brooks described preaching in that memorable phrase, "truth through personality." For there to be real preaching, he insisted, "The truth must come really through the person, not merely over his lips . . . through his character, his affections, his whole intellectual and moral being."[25]

Preaching is most fruitful when the message proclaimed is embodied in the messenger. Thus to preach Christ—incarnate, crucified, risen, exalted and coming again—we must be pervaded and possessed by him, participating ourselves in the very movements of the story we are proclaiming.

When this happens, then our preaching will fulfill its ultimate purpose: to magnify Jesus Christ. That means, according to Robert Smith Jr., a contemporary professor of homiletics, "not literally to make Him bigger" but "to present Him in such a way that the hearers see Him in a more glorious, majestic, holy, sovereign, just, faithful, and mighty manner than they have ever seen Him before."[26]

May the chapters that follow contribute toward that end. *Solus Christus!*

2

PREACHING
THE INCARNATION

He spoke the Incarnation and then so was born the Son
His final word was Jesus, He needed no other one.
Spoke flesh and blood so He could bleed and make a way Divine.
And so was born the baby who would die to make it mine.

Michael Card

As a young pastor, I wondered how I would be able to find something new and different to say each year at Christmas. However, I soon discovered I would never be able to exhaust the depth and the richness of the material. Numerous Old Testament texts (e.g., Is 9:6; 11:1-3; Mal 3:1-3; 4:1-3) speak prophetically of a coming Messiah, and a distinctive cast of Gospel characters—Mary and Joseph, Elizabeth and Zechariah, Anna and Simeon, shepherds and wise men, Herod and John the Baptist—all have significant lessons to teach us.

There are animals and angels, a Magnificat and a manger, genealogies and gifts, a wondrous star in the east and a violent slaughter of innocents, to say nothing of a newborn baby king. Thumb through Raymond Brown's magisterial *The Birth of the Messiah*, a 570-page commentary on the infancy narratives in Matthew and

Luke, and you'll never again worry about running out of ideas for Christmas sermons.

THE WORD MADE FLESH

Our problem, then, during Advent and Christmas, is not that we have too little to preach about. Our problem is that because there is so much, we can easily miss the main point of the story. Failing to "see the forest for the trees," we can easily neglect the heart of the Christmas message: the fact and significance of the incarnation. We sing about it every Advent season: "Joy to the world, the Lord has come!" "O come, O come, Emmanuel," "Veiled in flesh the Godhead see, hail the Incarnate Deity," "Word of the Father now in flesh appearing." But how often and how well do we preach about the miracle of Christmas?

For this is the most stupendous, astounding claim of all—that the baby lying in Bethlehem's manger is none other than the second person of the triune God. As J. I. Packer explains,

> It is here, in the thing that happened at the first Christmas that the profoundest and most unfathomable depths of the Christian revelation lie. "The Word was made flesh" (John 1:14); God became man; the divine Son became a Jew; the Almighty appeared on earth as a helpless human baby, unable to do more than lie and stare and wriggle and make noises, needing to be fed and changed and taught to talk like any other child. . . . The more you think about it, the more staggering it gets. Nothing in fiction is as fantastic as is this truth of the Incarnation.[1]

Think for a moment what it means. The One who inhabits eternity dwells in space and time, without ceasing to be eternal. The Creator comes to us as a creature in the world he has made, while remaining the creator and sustainer of all things. The Source of all human beings becomes a particular human being, while continuing to be the divine being. God the Son became human without ceasing to be divine. He became what he was not, while remaining what he always was. In the fourth century, Athanasius expressed it in a way that has never been improved upon: "The Word was not hedged in by His body, nor did His presence in the body prevent His being present elsewhere as well. . . . At one and the same time—this is the wonder—as Man he was living a human life, and as Word He was sustaining the life of the Universe, and as Son He was in constant union with the Father."[2]

Of course, we will never be able to fully comprehend or explain the "how" of the incarnation. Our finest attempts to fathom it always fall short, and the mystery remains. In the face of it, our most appropriate response is adoration. Charles Wesley's eighteenth-century hymn captures it well:

See in the infant's face
The depths of Deity
And labour while ye gaze,
To found the mystery;
In vain; ye angels gaze no more,
But fall and silently adore.[3]

In our own time, songwriter Michael Card expresses it like this:

No fiction as fantastic and wild
A mother made by her own child,
The hopeless babe who cried
Was God Incarnate and man deified.

This is the Mystery!
More than you can see.
Give up on your pondering
And fall down on your knees.[4]

How fitting then, that during Advent and Christmas, we come to "*adore* him, Christ the Lord."

The mystery of the incarnation is at the heart and center of the Christian faith. And though an awareness of mystery is common in all religions, this particular mystery—that the Word was made flesh—is found nowhere except in Christianity. In the fifth century, Augustine wrote in his *Confessions* that in his pre-Christian days he had read and studied the writings of all the great pagan philosophers, but none had ever said, "The Word became flesh." Such a notion—that God would assume a human body—had never crossed their minds. It is an idea, Augustine concluded, utterly unique to Christianity.[5]

Fifteen hundred years later, after spending over half a century as a missionary and evangelist in India where he was continually dialoguing with and witnessing to Hindus, Buddhists and Muslims, E. Stanley Jones came to the same conclusion: "This verse—'The Word became flesh' is the Great Divide. In all other religions it is Word became word—a philosophy, a moralism, a system, a technique." Only in Christianity "for all time and all men everywhere, 'the Word became flesh'—the Idea became Fact."[6]

The incarnation, then, distinguishes the Christian faith from all other faiths. But how do we preach it? How do we proclaim the incarnation?

Of course, the things we've talked about so far—the nature, mystery and uniqueness of the incarnation event—are foundational. But I believe the *significance* of the incarnation, not these things, should be our main focus of our preaching. "The Word became human and lived here on earth among us" (Jn 1:14)—that's the stupendous, stranger-than-fiction truth our faith is based upon. But what does it mean? Why does it matter? What difference does it make in our personal and communal lives? How does it determine what we do as a congregation and how we go about it? These are the questions we should be most concerned about. In what follows, then, let's try to answer them.

IDENTIFICATION AT ITS FULLEST

The incarnation means that at a particular place and time, God, the mastermind and maker of the whole dazzling universe, became a particular human being in order to fully experience and fully identify with the human condition. John says that "the Word became *human*" (Jn 1:14, italics mine). That means he assumed not generic humanity but a particular human body. He took it on, not merely as an outer garment he would later cast aside, but as his true form and figure. Max Lucado captures it well: "He who was larger than the universe became an embryo. . . . God was given eyebrows, elbows, two kidneys and a spleen. He stretched against the walls and floated in the amniotic fluids of his mother."[7] What an amazing act of divine condescension and identification it was!

He was born, like every human baby that has ever come into this world, at such-and-such a place and such-and-such a time. He was bound to the process of human development. He weighed so many pounds and was so many inches tall.

He had physical needs. He got hungry, thirsty and tired. He was susceptible to infections and colds. He burped and had body odor. He experienced the full range of human emotions: disappointment, loneliness, sorrow, anxiety, fear, anger, joy and happiness.

John declares that he "dwelt among us." Literally translated, the Greek states that he "pitched his tent" or "tabernacled" in our midst. Eugene Peterson's *Message* paraphrase reads that he "moved into our neighborhood." He was a part of a particular society and culture. Raised in Nazareth, an insignificant Galilean village, he spoke Aramaic with a thick, low-prestige accent. As a first-century Palestinian Jew, he felt the harsh cruelty and injustice of living under Roman occupation.

In 1962, the Christmas Day edition of the St. Petersburg, Florida, *Times* had two front pages. "In keeping with the Christmas spirit," the editor explained, "only good news will appear on the front page. For a full report on other happenings around the world, see page 3A."

So, true to his promise, the front page had only good news that day. There was a picture of the pope standing on the balcony blessing those gathered in St. Peter's square, a story of a church helping a needy family, another about pilgrims entering the gates of Bethlehem. And best of all, there was a large picture of Santa Claus, stretched out on a patio next to a swimming pool, with his boots off and toes wiggling in the warm Florida sunshine.

The other front page included the real headlines: Cuban freedom fighters retreat; masked gunmen grab $100,000 in Chicago; father and nine children perish in fire; civil war rages in Congo; government is overthrown in Tunisia.[8]

We can appreciate what the editor of the newspaper was attempting to do, but he missed the true meaning of Christmas. Jesus, the Son of God, wasn't born into a sentimental, good-news-only fantasy world. He was born into *this* world, *our* world, which was evil and dangerous then just as it is now. In his Gospel, Luke is careful to include the names of those who were ruling when Jesus was born: Emperor Augustus, Governor Quirinius and King Herod the Great (Lk 1:5; 2:1-2). All three were greedy, ruthless and cruel. The point is the Word became flesh and blood in a world of flesh and blood—cheap flesh and free-flowing blood.

This means that throughout his earthly existence God the Son experienced pain and suffering. For to really enter human history, to be born into our kind of world and to "dwell among us" is certainly a passport to pain. Throughout his human journey he knew suffering and hardship firsthand.

He was born in a smelly, insanitary stable, forced to flee as a refugee from his native country, raised in poverty, spurned by the religious establishment, run out of his hometown, misunderstood by his family, betrayed by one of his own disciples and executed as a common criminal. We could go on and on, but the point is, from the cradle to the cross, for Jesus to live was to suffer. David Bryant sums it up well: "Unprotected and vulnerable in His humanity, Jesus entered directly into our own painful frustrations, engaged our precarious conditions, tasted our futilities, and embraced our despairs."[9]

This means that God has not only *spoken* to us through a Son (Heb 1:2); he has also *listened* to us. He has shared in the fellowship of our sufferings and heard our cries. Through the incarnation—and by that we mean not just the miraculous initial moment when the Word became flesh, but the whole course of Christ's obedient life—his identification with humanity was complete. He fully entered into and experienced the human condition, eyeball to eyeball, heart to heart, hurt to hurt. No wonder we call him Emmanuel, "God with us" (Is 7:14).

God, then, in the person of his Son, knows how we feel and fully understands us. His knowledge of our predicament is not distant, secondhand or theoretical, but direct, firsthand and personal. God is not a stoic Unmoved Mover but an empathic Fellow-Sufferer who understands. In his poem "On Another's Sorrow," William Blake expresses it like this:

> He doth give His joy to all;
> He becomes an infant small;
> He becomes a man of woe;
> He doth feel the sorrow too.
>
> Think not thou canst sigh a sigh
> And thy Maker is not by;
> Think not thou canst weep a tear
> And thy Maker is not near.[10]

Incarnation means that God has come near. Here is identification at its fullest. He sighs and groans and weeps with us. God fully understands our human predicament and therefore is able to help us. As the writer of Hebrews declares, "Since he himself has gone through suffering and temptation, he is able to help us when we are being tempted" (Heb 2:18). "Only the suffering God can help,"[11] wrote Dietrich Bonhoeffer from a Nazi prison cell. Because God through the Son became a man of sorrows and familiar with suffering (Is 53:3), he is able, wonderfully able, to help us.

We need to herald this good news during the Christmas season. The perennial question, "Does God really care?" has been answered through the incarnation with an emphatic Yes. God does know and does care! Our Emmanuel is one with us all the way from the womb to the tomb! Our Emmanuel can help!

God knows and understands the human condition, and because of the incarnation, *now we know that he knows.* "This High Priest of ours understands our weaknesses, for he faced all of the same testings we do" (Heb 4:15). And because we know that he knows, we are able to "come boldly to the throne of our gracious God. There we will receive his mercy, and we will find grace to help us when we need it most" (Heb 4:16).

IMPLICATIONS OF THE INCARNATION

We also need to draw out the implications that incarnational identification has for our lives and for congregations—the way Paul does, for example, when he's writing to the Philippians. In exhorting them to put away selfishness and strife and to work together in harmony and love, Paul implores them to adopt "the same attitude that Christ Jesus had" (Phil 2:5). Then the apostle goes on to describe the incredible downward descent of the incarnation: "Though he was God, he did not demand and cling to his rights as God. He made himself nothing; he took the humble position of a slave and appeared in human form. And in human form he obediently humbled himself even further by dying a criminal's death on a cross" (Phil 2:6-8). If God so humbled himself and identified with us, shouldn't we follow the same pattern and reflect the same attitude in our relationships with others?

God's incarnational method of identification has a message for the "Mars" husband, with his distinctively male perspective, learning to listen, understand and love his mystifying, incomprehensible "Venus" wife; for the Christian mother struggling to reach her resistant teenage daughter; for the high school teacher trying to connect with his apathetic students; for the extroverted, outgoing boss seeking to motivate a shy, introverted employee; for the Christian family wanting to reach out to the Muslims who have moved into their neighborhood. It speaks volumes to the members of a divided congregation, alienated from one another because of past misunderstandings and disagreements over plans for the future.

For that matter, it has much to say to us preachers about the very way we go about preaching it. Whereas, according to T. S. Eliot, the purpose of literature is to turn blood into ink, the purpose of preaching is just the opposite: to turn ink back into blood. Yet according to homiletics professor Clayton Schmit, that is exactly what so many preachers fail to do. They "speak only abstractly, as if they were devoid of humanness. There's no flesh, no blood, no tension, no mystery, no life in their sermons. No dialogue, no communication, and no eye contact with those looking at them expectantly every Sunday morning. Only words drawn from commentaries or a thesaurus."[12] Such preaching is a denial of the incarnation. The Word became flesh and dwelt among us. The words of our sermons must take on flesh too.

Think also of the far-reaching implications the incarnation has for how we engage in mission. To communicate the gospel we can't do it from a distance or a place of superiority or power. We have to move into the neighborhood too! When over time we truly identify with people and they identify with us, then the message of the gospel breaks through. Then they begin to understand that God understands and cares.

A wonderful example of the power of incarnational identification comes to us from the life of George W. Harley, the pioneer missionary doctor who founded the Ganta Mission in 1926 in Liberia, Africa. Called by some "Methodism's Albert Schweitzer in Africa," Harley grew up in North Carolina and was trained and educated at Duke, Yale and London universities. When he and his wife, Winifred, arrived in Liberia, some thought that because of his qualifications, they would make him chief of staff at the Harvey Firestone Memorial Hospital in the capital city of Monrovia. But the Harleys felt called to establish a mission station in the interior.

So with the help of native guides they set out toward Ganta, the principal village among the 600,000 people of the Mano tribe, located at the edge of the forest 150 miles inland. Seven days later after a difficult journey—much of the time they had to cut their way through the bush—they arrived at their destination. The residents of Ganta were friendly and helped the Harleys build several huts. One was to be a medical dispensary, another a chapel and another their home. And so the Ganta Mission Station was established in the interior of Africa. Years later one of the finest hospitals in Liberia was built there. The station still exists today and is being rebuilt after being attacked by rebel missiles during the 2003 civil war.

In a matter of months after the Harleys' arrival at Ganta, the white doctor's fame had spread throughout the tiny villages of the forest, and sick people were pouring into the dispensary for treatment. Less than eighteen months later, Harley wrote home describing it like this: "Ask some young doctor in your neighborhood who has had his office open just one year how many patients he had yesterday. Then tell him that yesterday I had 160."[13] Eventually he would treat over 10,000 people each year.

Yet although they received his medical help gladly, the Mano were reticent to receive the gospel of Christ or to accept the Christian faith. That would only begin to happen after George and Winifred had been there about five years. One evening years later when the Harleys were on furlough in the U.S., they were having dinner with Kenneth Goodson, a Methodist pastor from North Carolina who would later become a bishop. During their conversation, Harley told Goodson about the breakthrough that created an openness to the gospel among the Mano.

Shortly after they had arrived at Ganta, Winifred gave birth to the Harleys' first child, a baby boy. "We named him Robert and called him Bobby, and he grew up there on the edge of the forest," Harley told Goodson. "He was the apple of our eye. How we loved our little boy!

"But then one day when he was almost five years old, I looked out the window of the medical dispensary and saw Bobby. He was running across the field but he fell down. Then he got up and ran some more and fell again. But this time he didn't get up. So I ran out and picked up the feverish body of my own little boy. I held him in my arms and said, 'Bobby, don't worry. Your daddy knows how to treat that tropical fever. He's going to help you get better.'

"So I pulled out all the stops, I tried every treatment I knew. But one night, a few days later, as the fever continued to rage, I accepted what I was afraid of from the beginning. And the next morning, our little Bobby was dead.

"So I went down to the wood shop and made a little coffin, and we laid Bobby in it. After I had nailed on the lid, I lifted the coffin and put it on my shoulders and started down to the clearing to find a spot where I could bury my son. To get there I had to go near the village. When one of the old men in the village saw me he said, 'What are you doing? Where are you going with that box?'

" 'My son has died,' I told him, 'I'm going to bury him.' And the old man said, 'Here, let me help you.'

"You know, Ken," George Harley interjected, "I had lived next to that village for five years and no one had ever come to the chapel. I had preached every Sunday, but only Winifred and Bobby were there. They let me minister to their bodies, but they weren't interested in the gospel. To them Christianity was a foreign religion. It was for the white man, not for them."

Then Harley continued, "So the old man took one end of the coffin and I took the other. Eventually we came to the clearing in the forest. We dug a grave there and laid Bobby in it. But when we had covered up the grave, I just couldn't stand it any longer. My grief was so intense, my heart was breaking, I fell down on my knees in the dirt and began to sob uncontrollably. My beloved son was dead, and there I was in the middle of an African jungle 8,000 miles from home and relatives. I felt so all alone.

"But when I started crying, the old man cocked his head in stunned amazement. He squatted down beside me and looked at me so intently. For a long time, he sat there listening to me cry. Then suddenly, he leaped to his feet and went running back up the trail through the jungle, screaming, again and again, at the top of his voice, 'White man, white man—he cries like one of us.'

"That evening Winifred and I were sitting at the table. Everything within us was breaking up. We were ready to leave Ganta and return home. Then we heard a knock, and when I opened the door, there stood the chief and behind him was almost every man, woman, and child in the village.

"The next Sunday morning, they were back again. The chapel was filled and many were outside looking in the windows. They wanted to hear the gospel, to learn about Jesus, and I knew we had finally broken through."

In redeeming lost humanity and fallen creation, incarnational identification was God's own missionary method. To break through, the Word, who was with God and was God, became flesh and dwelt among us. He cried like one of us. When we go forth in his name, as George Harley came to understand, such identification must be our method as well. Lao Tsu, the ancient Chinese poet, captured the essence of it centuries ago:

> Go to the people
> Live among them,
> Learn from them,
> Love them.
> Start with what they know,
> Build on what they have.[14]

That's what God did. Wherever we are called to go—whether it is to our family, workplace, congregation, community, city, nation or world—we must go and do likewise. And what specifically will that look like? We must not rest, but keep reflecting and praying and grappling until we find out.

REVELATION AT ITS CLEAREST

"No one has ever seen God," says the apostle John (Jn 1:18). Even when Moses asked if he could, he was firmly told, "You can't see my face and live." As a sign of his special favor, however, God hid Moses in the cleft of a rock and passed by so he could see his back (Ex 33:20-23). Earlier when the elders of Israel "saw the God of Israel," they only viewed the pavement under his feet (Ex 24:9-10). Likewise, when the prophet Isaiah "saw the Lord" he merely glimpsed the hem of God's robe (Is 6:1). In each instance, the Hebrew writer uses anthropomorphic language to convey that God is so radically different from us, so totally other, all our attempts to fully understand or grasp or describe this Holy One are futile and doomed to failure. As theologian Emil Brunner reminds us, "The border line which separates the nature of God from all other forms of existence . . . is not only a frontier line, it is a closed frontier."[15]

God is not one thing among others, nor can God be positively compared to any created thing whether it is an archangel, an aard-

vark, an ant or an amoeba. We can't even say that God exists in the
same way we say a mountain or an animal or a human being exists, for God is existence itself, the reality out of which all other
realities arise. Left to ourselves, we can only be certain about what
God is not.

If then we are to know anything positive about God with any
degree of clarity or certainty, God alone must take the initiative
and make himself known to us. Through the incarnation, John
declares, that is exactly what God has done. Although no one has
seen God, the only Son, who is near to the Father's heart, has
made him known to us (Jn 1:18).

This too is the message we must proclaim at Christmas: The
Word who was God and was with God (Jn 1:1), having become
flesh and dwelt among us (Jn 1:14), has revealed God to us (Jn
1:18). God has not left us futilely searching, crying out like Job,
"Oh that I knew where I might find him" (Job 23:3 KJV). God has
come down to us and been disclosed in the person of his Son. In
the words of John Calvin: "It is not necessary for us to mount up
on high to inquire about what must be hidden from us at this moment. For God lowers himself to us. He shows us only in his Son—
as though he says, 'Here I am. Contemplate me.'"[16]

A young boy born into a wealthy family in Victorian England
was devastated with grief and loneliness when his father suddenly
died. A large oil painting of the father hung in the well-furnished
drawing room of his home. One day the boy's mother observed
him as he stood in front of it, gazing sadly at the painted figure of
his father. "Daddy," she heard him say, "how I wish you would
come down out of that frame and speak to me!" Consciously or
unconsciously, that has been the cry of all humanity to God—
until Jesus came and emphatically declared, "Anyone who has
seen me has seen the Father" (Jn 14:9).

In the face of Jesus Christ we have truly seen the face of God.
As Paul emphatically declared, "In Christ the fullness of God lives

in a human body" (Col 2:9). Here, then, is the revelation of God at its clearest. We need never look elsewhere to discover what God is like, nor do we ever need go behind Christ or beyond Christ. The full and final disclosure of God is found in him.

Scottish theologian Thomas Torrance tells how as a young army chaplain he held the hand of a dying nineteen-year-old soldier on a World War II battlefield. "Will God really turn out to be like Jesus?" he desperately wanted to know. Years later while pastoring a church in Scotland, he visited one of the oldest women in his congregation, who asked him the very same question. Torrance gladly assured them both "that God is indeed really like Jesus, and that there is no unknown God behind the back of Jesus for us to fear; to see the Lord Jesus is to see the very face of God."[17] Surely, that is good news for all who struggle with distorted pictures and misconceptions of God.

For Christians, then, the most significant question is not, What is God like? but, Is God Christlike? And to that question our answer is an unequivocal and resounding Yes. As Torrance sums it up in another place, "Jesus Christ constitutes in his own incarnate Person the mediating center of that revelation whereby all our knowledge of God is controlled."[18]

But the incarnate Christ reveals not only what *God* is like; by becoming fully human, he also reveals what *human beings,* according to God's original design and intention, are meant to be. Humanity was originally created in the image of God (Gen 1:26). However, because of our fall into sin through Adam, the divine image in us was defaced almost beyond recognition. The incarnation, then, marks a crucial point in the great restoration, for in Christ we see the image of God displayed in full splendor once again. As Emil Brunner states, "the fact that man is 'made in the image of God' is only fully disclosed in this divine act of the incarnation."[19] In keeping with this, the New Testament explicitly states in several places that Christ himself is the image of God

(2 Cor 4:4; Col 1:15; Heb 1:3). The process and the goal of Christian formation is also described as being renewed in the image of God (Col 3:10) and conformed to the image of his Son (Rom 8:29).

The model of human personhood Jesus lived out also provides the foundation for an authentic Christian humanism—one that has much more to offer than the various forms of humanism being advocated in North America and other parts of the world today. Why not, then, lift up the life of the incarnate Christ as the revelation of what humanity, created in God's image, is supposed to be? In a culture that urges us to "be all that you can be," doesn't Jesus provide an alternative yet most attractive model of what that means? Aren't his answers to the deepest human questions—about the nature of human freedom, hope, dignity, self-identity and self-esteem—much better than the ones being peddled by Oprah Winfrey, Deepak Chopra or Dr. Phil?

In the incarnate Christ we thus see revelation at its clearest. He is the full and final disclosure both of what God is like and what we are meant to be. That's why as Christians we always begin and end with him. E. Stanley Jones sums it up insightfully:

Christianity is Christ. . . . We do not begin with God, for if you do you do not begin with God but with your ideas of God, which are not God. We do not begin with man, for if you do you begin with the problems of man. And if you begin with a problem you will probably end with a problem, and in the process you will probably become a problem. . . . We don't begin with God, and we don't begin with man, we begin with the God-Man and from Him we work out to God, and from Him we work down to man. In His light we see life—all life. For He is the revelation of God and man—the revelation of what God is and what man can become—he can become Christlike.[20]

SHOW AND TELL

In the incarnation, revelation is at its clearest not only in terms of *content;* it is also clearest because of its *form.* A scientist making a plea for exchange scholarships between nations said that "the best way to export an idea is to wrap it up in a person."[21] In the incarnation that's exactly what God did. He revealed himself not through a word or an act, as he had often done before, but through a concrete, historical human person—one that, as John emphasizes, we could see with our eyes, hear with our ears and touch with our hands (1 Jn 1:1-3). He came to us in an embodied form, the form best suited for human comprehension.

According to the writer of Hebrews, throughout salvation history God had spoken to his people in various times and ways through the prophets (Heb 1:1). In the incarnation, however, God moved beyond the Old Testament form of revelation, speaking to us instead through a Son (Heb 1:2)—a divine-human person, an embodied person in whom word and deed, speech and act, are perfectly conjoined. In former times, people had seen God act and heard God speak. But his words and deeds were distinct and separate. Divine revelation was either show *or* tell. Now, however, in the coming of Jesus it is show *and* tell. Everything he preaches, he embodies; ideas are wrapped up in a person. In the incarnate Christ, God himself in person is present, both speaking and acting.

We live in an increasingly virtual world of Facebook, Twitter and smart phones. Certainly these and other forms of digital communication technology have their place and enable us to stay connected to people at certain levels. Yet though they move us beyond the impersonal, in the light of the incarnation, they simply aren't personal enough. God desires not only to communicate but to commune with us. To accomplish that, only face-to-face, person-to-person encounter will do. God so loved the world that he did not text, tweet or post a message on Facebook. Instead God gave his only Son, "born of a woman, born under the law" (Gal 4:4 NRSV).

Because we are personal beings by nature, the most appropriate form of revelation for us is the personal. When embodied in persons, principles become compelling. That's what God did in the incarnation: he came as a baby in a manger. In his missionary classic *The Christ of the Indian Road,* published in 1925, E. Stanley Jones eloquently portrays the powerful difference Christ's show-and-tell, personal revelation made:

> He did not discourse on the sacredness of motherhood—he suckled as a babe at his mother's breast and that scene has forever consecrated motherhood. . . .
>
> He did not discourse on the dignity of labor—he worked at a carpenter's bench and his hands were hard with the toil of making yokes and plows, and this forever makes the toil of the hands honorable. . . .
>
> He did not teach in a didactic way about the worth of children—he put his hands upon them and blessed them and setting one in their midst tersely said, "Of such is the kingdom of God." . . .
>
> He did not paint in glowing colors the beauties of friendship and the need for human sympathy—he wept at the grave of a friend.
>
> He did not argue the worth of womanhood and the necessity of giving them equal rights—he treated them with infinite respect, gave to them his most sublime teaching, and when he arose from the dead he appeared first to a woman.
>
> He did not teach in the schoolroom manner the necessity of humility—he "girded himself with a towel and kneeled down and washed his disciples' feet."[22]

This personal form of revelation that comes to us in the incarnation has profound implications for Christian ministry and mission. The truth of the gospel is most convincing when it's embodied in a person or a community of persons. When people see it lived out in our lives, concretely taking shape in our life together, embodied in both our words and actions, they are much more apt to believe.

In *The Shaping of Things to Come,* written to help the church engage in mission in the twenty-first century, authors Michael Frost and Alan Hirsch devote four chapters to developing an "incarnational ecclesiology." In one of those chapters, Frost tells of a talkback session at an evangelistic rally he attended in Sydney, Australia. Following his address, the evangelist who had preached was answering questions submitted by members of the audience. Since most were questions he had heard before, his answers were rapid and smoothly recited. Then came a question no one was expecting: "Where was God when I was raped?" You could hear a pin drop in the auditorium as everyone wondered what the evangelist would say.

Frost describes what happened next: "The evangelist paused, then attempted to reply. . . . Each time he leaned toward the microphone to answer, he couldn't bring himself to speak. Then big salty tears began to stream down his face. He couldn't speak because of the lump in his throat. He wept openly on the platform that night. . . . When later he had composed himself he raged against a patriarchal society that gives men the assumed permission to see women as objects."[23]

Frost says he can't remember any of the evangelist's polished answers to the questions posed at the rally. But he has never forgotten the evangelist's compassion for the woman who had asked where God was when she was raped. Frost concludes, "He was epitomized in those salty tears and that anger at violence and oppression."[24] Whenever something like this happens, where gospel truth is not just spoken, but embodied in a living person, it makes a profound impact on us.

During the Christmas season, we need to challenge our congregations to adopt God's incarnational method where word and flesh combine, where ideas are wrapped up in persons. That was God's way of bringing us revelation at its clearest. It must be our way too.

REDEMPTION AT ITS FINEST

I purchased my first computer in the mid-1980s but still remember the days when I used an electric typewriter. Sometimes in beginning to compose, I would get frustrated after I had typed several sentences or paragraphs. Shaking my head I would think to myself, *This just isn't going to work. I need to start over.* So in one continuous motion, I'd grab the paper, rip it out of the typewriter carriage, wad it up in a ball and then hurl it at the waste-basket over in the corner. Compared to simply pushing a delete button on a computer, there was something much more authentic, gutsy, stress-reducing and satisfying about that!

After God created human beings, he almost decided to start over too. Adam and Eve had disobeyed his command and were banished from the Garden of Paradise. By the time of Noah, things had gone from bad to a whole lot worse. So much so that when the Lord "observed the extent of the people's wickedness," he "saw that all their thoughts were consistently and totally evil" and he was "sorry he had ever made them. It broke his heart" (Gen 6:5-6). Then God sent a great flood to wipe them all out—except for Noah and his family, who "found favor with the LORD" (Gen 6:8). Later the Lord made a covenant with Noah "never to send another flood to kill all the living creatures and destroy the earth" (Gen 9:11). The rainbow God placed in the sky was a sign of that covenant.

God, then, could have decided to start over, and almost did. The Lord could have said, "Plan A didn't work, let's try Plan B." But God chose not to. God decided to stick with his original plan and not give up on humanity altogether. Later, the covenants God made with Abraham, Moses and the people of Israel, and King David were all evidence of his continued commitment to humanity.

Through the incarnation, God took the ultimate step in that commitment. He affirmed humanity by actually becoming human. In the words of Thomas Aquinas, "God has now shown us the high place human nature holds in creation, for he entered into it by genuinely becoming man."[25]

In the incarnation, God assumes human nature itself, joins himself to it, and not merely in an episodic or temporary fashion, but, as we shall especially see when we consider the ascension, *for all eternity*. The incarnation therefore secures the knowledge, as Emil Brunner states, that "God's will is wholly a will for humanity."[26]

We need to stress this in our preaching because negative views of the material, the body and the human in general are still propagated in many Christian circles. Often the material is set over against the spiritual, the body is portrayed as the enemy of the spirit, and the human is viewed as an obstacle to the divine. As John Stott observes, there is a "lingering evangelical asceticism" rooted in a "world-denying Gnosticism" that "has not yet been altogether eradicated from our theology and practice."[27]

To be sure, humanity is radically fallen. The unredeemed flesh is sinful and hostile to God (Gal 5:17) and therefore must be put to death in us (Rom 8:13). Nevertheless, by sending his own Son in the likeness of sinful flesh (Rom 8:3), by dwelling among us in human form, God has, in Charles Williams's wonderful phrase, "forever hallowed the flesh" and declared the final verdict on fallen human nature: God intends to redeem and restore it to its original created purpose.

Through the incarnation, God who is Spirit becomes an embodied human being. Spirit does not despise matter. That's why Christianity, as Archbishop William Temple was fond of saying, is the most materialistic religion in the world. For not only did God

create the material world and call it good, but when it had become
corrupted by humanity's sin, God assumed matter by sending his
own Son in a human body like ours in order to redeem and restore
matter. Every time we affirm with the Apostles' Creed, "I believe
in the resurrection of the body," we are, in effect, declaring that.
God intends to redeem our bodies, the material side of our existence, as well as our souls and spirits.

True Christian spirituality therefore celebrates the material
dimensions of creaturely existence. It is an *earthy* spirituality. Dietrich Bonhoeffer was concerned that well-intentioned Christians
often drove an erroneous, unbiblical wedge between the sacred
and the secular, the spiritual and the material, the heavenly and
the earthly. "I fear that Christians who stand with only one leg on
earth," he wrote from Tegel prison, "also stand with only one leg
in heaven."[28] The incarnation summons us to fix both legs on
earth in order that both may also be fixed in heaven. We should be
able to enjoy feasting as well as engage in fasting, to play hard and
work hard, to celebrate our sexuality and seek after sanctity.

Recognizing God's affirmation of the human in the incarnation
also forms the basis of an authentic and robust Christian humanism. If God so values the human that he joins himself to it by becoming flesh, can we think of valuing it less? Do we dare call
"unclean" what God has called "clean"? Thomas Merton spells out
this connection well:

> If the Word of God assumed a human nature and became a
> man, in all things like other men except sin, if he gave his life
> to unite the human race to God in his Mystical Body, then
> surely there must be an authentic humanism which is not
> only acceptable to Christians but is essential to the Christian
> mystery itself. . . . In defending the natural law, the civic rights
> of men, the rights of human reason, the cultural values of di-
> verse civilizations, scientific study and technics, medicine,

political science and a thousand other good things in the natural order, the Church is expressing her profoundly Christian humanism, or, in other words, her concern for man in all his wholeness and integrity as a creature and as the image of God. . . . The salvation of man does not mean that he must divest himself of all that is human: that he must discard his reason, his love of beauty, his desire for friendship, his need for human affection, his reliance on protection, order, and justice in society, his need to work and eat and sleep.

A Christianity that despises these fundamental needs of man is not truly worthy of the name.[29]

The incarnation, then, calls us to work for the protection and advancement of all that is truly human. No wonder the angels announced, "And on earth peace, good will toward men" (Lk 2:14 KJV). Advent is a season to spell out the implications of that and to call our congregations to participate in God's efforts to redeem humanity.

WE CAN BE TRANSFORMED
The incarnation indeed signals God's affirmation of humanity; it also tells us that we can be redeemed, transformed, changed in a way that previously wasn't possible for fallen sinners. Through Christ we can be reconciled and restored to God. We can experience renewed relationship with God, a union with the triune God characterized by joyful intimacy and trust. "Having become what we are," wrote Gregory of Nyssa, "He through Himself again united humanity to God."[30]

The Son of God became flesh and lived out within our fallen, perverted human existence the true life of humanity created after God in righteousness and holiness. In all that he thought and willed and did, Jesus lived out among humanity a life of utter obedience and faithfulness to the Father. He was thus the perfect

image of God on earth, and in him the way is opened for humanity
to be restored to communion with God. In another of his Christmas hymns, Charles Wesley expresses it like this:

> He deigns in flesh to appear,
> Widest extremes to join;
> To bring our vileness near,
> And make us all divine,
> And we the life of God shall know,
> For God is manifest below.[31]

Theologian William Placher[32] describes the various images
Christian theologians in the third and fourth centuries used to
explain the transformation now possible because of the life of God
in us. Cyril of Alexandria said that by assuming flesh, like the
cloth dye that adds color and beauty to our clothes, Christ had
dyed the human soul with the divine nature. Athanasius and Hi-
lary compared humanity to a city where a king resides. Just as all
of the citizens of the city receive special care, honor and benefits
because the king lives there, so all of us are blessed because divinity was united with humanity in one of our fellow human beings.
Gregory of Nazianzus said it was like the effect of the sun's rays in
the morning. It burns off the fog and then changes the quality of
the air as sunlight fills it.

The Eastern church uses the word *theosis* ("deification") to describe the transformation made possible by the incarnation, citing
2 Peter 1:4, which speaks of our "sharing in his divine nature."
The Divine Word became human, it often says, so that humanity
could be made divine. Of course, *theosis,* as T. F. Torrance explains, doesn't mean "divinization," as if somehow we become
gods and are no longer fully human. Instead what Eastern theologians are underscoring is "the utterly staggering act of God in
which he gives *himself* to us, and *adopts us* into the communion of
his divine life and love . . . yet in such a way that we are not made

divine but are preserved in our humanity."[33] Likewise, Donald Fairbairn, in presenting the Eastern view, stresses that *theosis* is not about participation in the divine substance or essence, but "participation in a relationship,"[34] the relationship the Son has with the Father, and sharing in the love they have for each other.

Despite such clarifications, many Western theologians have shied away from using *theosis* or deification language to describe the transformation the incarnation makes possible. They have preferred the language of adoption instead. As John puts it immediately before he declares that the Word became flesh: "But to all who believed him and accepted him, he gave the right to become children of God" (Jn 1:12). So Western theologians have said that the second person of the Trinity, who was a Son by nature, became human so that we might become sons and daughters by adoption.

Perhaps the truth lies somewhere between East and West. I like the word C. S. Lewis used to describe the change: *transposition,* where a lower reality is actually drawn into a higher one and becomes a part of it. Through the incarnation, he suggests, "Humanity, still remaining itself, is not merely counted as, but veritably drawn into, Deity."[35]

Yet regardless of the language we use to describe it, all Christians agree that the reality of the transformation and union with God through Christ, both embodied in and made possible by the incarnation, is profound and glorious. Because Christ has become human, what it means to be human has changed for everyone. Our sin had cut us off from God. Through the incarnation God reestablished contact with us and created the possibility of a humanity reconciled, restored and united to God.

Placher sums it up well: "When the word became flesh, what it means to be human changed for each of us—you, me, Hitler, the bag lady, and the heroin addict huddled on a street corner on a winter night—because in one human being humanity was united with divinity."[36] Something tells me that will preach!

3

PREACHING THE CROSS

SCANDAL, ATONEMENT, SUFFERING, LOVE

The cross of Christ is a many-splendoured thing.
Like a diamond, it has many shining facets.
And the preacher is charged with the responsibility
of holding those facets up to the gaze of the congregation.

MICHAEL GREEN

One of the most remarkable works of religious art to appear in recent times (1951) is Salvador Dali's painting *Christ of St. John of the Cross*. When it was displayed in the National Gallery in London in 2000, fifty thousand people lined up to see it. A press report described its impact this way: "Men entering the room where the picture is hung instinctively take off their hats. Crowds of chattering, high-spirited school children are hushed into awed silence when they see it."[1] When I was visiting Scotland in May 2003, I was privileged to view it myself in the Glasgow art gallery where it normally hangs.

Unlike more familiar presentations of the crucifixion where the cross is viewed from ground level, in Dali's painting the cross is viewed from above, as if one were viewing it from heaven, from

God's perspective. The cross in the picture is massive; it looms over the whole world beneath. The figure on the cross is young and strong. He seems to be holding back the darkness surrounding him. In the foreground, the earth, the sky and the sea are illumined by the light streaming forth from the cross. The whole world is viewed from the cross, and how different it looks from that perspective!

Preachers, too, should help their hearers view everything from the vantage point of the cross. For the cross truly is at the very heart of everything distinctively Christian. That's why it is the primary identifying sign, the chief visual symbol of the Christian faith. No wonder that Christian art, architecture, literature and hymns have been so dominated by it. Alister McGrath says it well: "The cross of Christ is the point of reference for Christian faith; Christian faith is based upon it, and judged by it. . . . Christian theology, Christian worship, and Christian ethics are essentially nothing other than an attempt to explore and develop the meaning and implications of the crucified Christ in every area of life."[2]

Often we have proclaimed only one dimension of the cross (e.g., "Christ died to save us from our sins"), but that simply won't do. Like the New Testament writers, we too must communicate its many-splendored message. Drawing from their ancient Jewish and Greco-Roman contexts, they used a wide variety of images and metaphors to convey the significance of Christ's death. In sorting out this "kaleidoscope of images," New Testament scholar Joel Green shows how they generally revolve around five spheres of public life: the court of law (justification), the world of commerce (redemption), personal relationships (reconciliation), worship (sacrifice) and battleground (triumph over evil).[3] Each sheds light on a different consequence of sin that the cross addresses.

We too must proclaim the cross from a variety of perspectives in order to demonstrate its profound relevance to a wide range of human need. So in this chapter and the next I hope to paint in

broad strokes the main themes, the big ideas we need to accentu-
ate in our preaching of the cross.

RECOVERING THE SCANDAL OF THE CROSS

In the American church and in our culture in general, we are so
accustomed to seeing crosses on church buildings or in sanctuar-
ies, wearing them on chains, or carrying them in processions that
it's virtually impossible for us to grasp the utter horror the very
mention of crucifixion provoked in the ancient world. "Do you
sell gold crosses?" a customer inquired in the jewelry section of a
Denver, Colorado, department store. "What kind would you like?"
asked the clerk, as she pulled out one of the trays. "A plain one or
one that has the little man on it?" For us, the cross is an endear-
ing, often sentimental, religious symbol that evokes positive feelings, or perhaps no feelings at all.

Not so when the apostles originally proclaimed the message of
the cross. Far from being a *religious* symbol, the cross was shock-
ing, revolting and offensive, a disgusting *irreligious* symbol if there
ever was one.

Since most modern hearers are largely unaware of that, we must
be intentional in making what has become so familiar strange
again, helping them recover the scandal of the cross (1 Cor 1:23).
Here's how Fleming Rutledge does that in one of her sermons:

> Not even the celebrated film by Mel Gibson, *The Passion of
> the Christ,* can convey the full ghastliness of crucifixion to a
> modern audience. We don't understand it because we have
> never seen anything like it in the flesh. The situation was
> very different in New Testament times. . . . Everyone knew
> what it looked like, smelled like, sounded like—the horrific
> sight of completely naked men in agony, the smell and sight
> of their bodily functions taking place in full view of all, the
> sounds of their groans and labored breathing going on for

hours and, in some cases, for days. Perhaps worst of all is the fact that no one cared.[4]

We tend to associate the horror of crucifixion with agonizing physical pain—what Mel Gibson so vividly portrayed in his film. That was a major dimension, and it's no accident that our English word *excruciating* is derived from *crux,* the Latin word for "cross." Yet despite the unbearable physical agony, people in Roman times dreaded the shame associated with crucifixion even more. Since crucifixion was reserved for the dregs of society, outcasts, slaves and common criminals, the fact that one was crucified defined him or her as a miserable, wretched being that didn't deserve to exist. By pinning them up like insects, crucifixion was deliberately intended to display and humiliate its victims.

It was always carried out in public, often at a prominent place such as a crossroads, outdoor theater or hill. Crucifixion was a spectacle event, a grisly form of entertainment where passersby jeered and heaped ridicule upon the victim. The public mockery of Jesus during his crucifixion (Mk 15:29-32) was typical. The shame of the crucified was compounded by their nakedness, as well as the fact that they were often denied burial and became food for vultures and other scavengers.

Crucifixion, then, was deliberately designed to be loathsome, vulgar, revolting and obscene. That's why, although common in Roman times, it was rarely mentioned in cultured literary or social settings. *Crux* was a four-letter word, not to be used in polite company. Cicero, one of Rome's greatest philosophers, said that no respectable person should ever have to hear it spoken.

The hideous shame associated with crucifixion was the main reason why the message of the cross seemed ludicrous to its original hearers. As Paul put it, "When we preach that Christ was crucified, the Jews are offended, and the Gentiles say it's all nonsense" (1 Cor 1:23). To proclaim that someone who was hanged on "the tree of shame"[5] was the Savior of the world or the long-awaited Messiah was bizarre and disgusting—sheer madness.

Alister McGrath likens the early Christian preaching of the cross to a modern business or corporation choosing a hangman's noose, lynching tree, firing squad, gas chamber or electric chair as its logo. What advertising agency would advise you to choose an instrument of execution as the recognition symbol for your organization? "Its members would instantly be regarded as perverted, sick, having a morbid obsession with death, or having a nauseating interest in human suffering. . . . Only an organization determined to fail as quickly and spectacularly as possible would be mad enough to choose such a symbol."[6]

However, by making it the centerpiece of their proclamation, that's exactly what the early Christians did. As Paul reminded the Corinthians, "When I first came to you I didn't use lofty words and brilliant ideas to tell you God's message. For I decided to concentrate only on Jesus Christ and his death on the cross" (1 Cor 2:1-2). Though it seemed strange and outlandish, they were convinced it was the supreme demonstration of the power and wisdom of God.

Preaching the scandal of the cross can help our congregations understand how God works to accomplish his redemptive purposes in the world. As the prophet declared, "My thoughts are completely different from yours . . . and my ways are far beyond anything you could imagine" (Is 55:8). The cross reveals that God's upside-down kingdom can be downright offensive to us. God uses that which the world considers despicable and weak to manifest his power. What does that say about our desiring strength as the world counts strength? Or our attempts to downplay or soften the offense of the cross?

OUTSIDE THE CAMP
The scandal of the cross also reveals who God takes sides with. By

allowing himself to be "counted among the rebels" (Is 53:12), crucified between two despicable criminals, God casts his lot with the poor, the powerless, the wretched, the dispossessed of the earth. Liberation theologians speak of God's "preferential option for the poor." What is seen throughout Scripture—God's concern for the helpless, the outcast, the widow, the orphan, the fatherless and the oppressed—is impossible to miss when the Son of God hangs on a cross between two thieves.

And of course, this has implications for the church. As the writer of Hebrews emphasizes, if he suffered "outside the city gates," in the garbage heap, the place of disgrace, among the reviled, "so let us go out to him outside the camp and bear the disgrace he bore" (Heb 13:13). We too are called to be involved with the lowest and the least, the outcasts, the despised and the dispossessed.

Once when I was pastoring in a small-town church, I found myself thinking about who those people would be in our particular community. *Who are the people in our town who tend to be looked upon as "outcasts"?* I wondered. *Those who are considered "outside the camp"?*

As I pondered, two groups of people came to mind. There was a home on one end of town for mentally challenged and older adults. For the most part, the residents there were not so disabled they had to be institutionalized. They were simply "throwaway" people whom nobody wanted, so they had been placed in the home either by their families or the state.

Most of them were not strictly confined to the home, so they were free to walk around town. Often people would interact with them on the streets or in the local stores. They were friendly and didn't create any problems in the community. However, town residents often laughed at them and made fun of them behind their backs.

The other group of people that came to my mind were the "druggies," as they were called—those in their late teens and early twenties who were regular and addicted drug users. They were loud, boisterous, dirty and unkempt. Most were unemployed. Some were stealing to support their drug habit. The people in that conservative, established little town viewed them with contempt. As far as they were concerned, the druggies were the scum of the community.

Several weeks later, I preached a sermon challenging our congregation about our need to love and minister to those "outside the camp," the place where Christ was crucified. You could hear a pin drop in the sanctuary when I specifically began to talk about the two groups of people I had been thinking about. "Christ is calling us as a congregation to spend time with these people and to think about ways we can reach out to them," I emphasized.

Then at the close of my sermon I issued a challenge: "If any of you can think of some concrete, practical ways we can begin ministering to these groups, get in touch with me. Let's talk. Let's see what we can come up with as we ask the Lord to show us how we can minister to these 'outcasts' of our community."

Immediately after the service, a middle-aged woman approached me. "I've been concerned about the people in that home too," she said. "I have a couple of afternoons a week when I'm off work. I also have experience doing craft programs with older adults. So I'd be willing to go to that home each week and start a craft program there."

"Go to it," I replied. "We'll get some others who'll assist you and help pay for craft materials."

In two weeks the program was up and running. The residents of the home were thrilled since nothing like that was being provided for them. They felt like someone genuinely cared. It wasn't long before some of them began showing up at our Sunday morning worship service.

Later in the week two young couples dropped by my office. "We've been concerned about the druggies for a long time," they said. "We were there once ourselves, and Jesus delivered us. They need to know he can do the same for them. So we were wondering if we could create a gathering place at the church on Friday nights where they can come and hang out, a place where they will feel welcome." At first some of the long-time members of the church were reluctant about the idea, but they agreed to do it on a trial basis. It wasn't long before that ministry was up and running too.

Needless to say I was thrilled and amazed at the response to my sermon. It also makes me wonder what might happen if in your preaching you helped your congregation grasp the scandal of the cross and challenged them to consider its implications. What profound things might begin to happen through your church?

THE GRAVITY OF SIN

If you were to ask a group of Christians to explain why Jesus had to die on the cross, they would no doubt respond, "To save us from our sins." Most Christians know there is a close connection between the cross and human sin. This connection is firmly rooted in the New Testament (e.g., 1 Cor 15:3; Heb 9:26; 1 Pet 3:18; 1 Jn 1:7; Rev 1:5).

But if you pressed the same group further, if you asked, "Why was his death necessary to accomplish that? Couldn't God have dealt with it some other way? How does the cross undo the problem of sin?" the majority would be unable to give you a coherent, satisfying answer. They can connect the cross with the problem of sin, but aren't sure how or why it provides the solution.

And the reason is quite simple. Jerome said that if you are going to understand the antidote, you must first understand the poison. Most Christians have a difficult time explaining why the death of Christ is the proper antidote for the poison of sin because they've never really come to grips with the poison. They know the right answer—Christ died for our sins—but when they speak it, the answer seems superficial, hollow, trite and unconvincing. And given the loss of the general awareness of sin in American culture over the past seventy-five years, coupled with the shift to post-modern relativism, the disconnect between the solution and the problem is growing.

The cross, then, is the answer to the problem of sin, but what do we do when very few people understand what the problem is or seem bothered by it? As we proclaim the biblical message that Christ died for our sins, such is the dilemma we face.

Let me suggest that in helping people come to grips with the reality and nature of sin, we let the antidote itself—the cross—define the poison. In fact, to properly understand both the poison and the antidote, the best thing we can do is invite people to stand at the foot of the cross. Like nothing else, the cross itself reveals, in Anselm's phrase, "what a heavy weight sin is." And like nothing else, the Christ reveals what God himself has done to remove the weight.

For at the cross we see Jesus, the incarnate Son of God, being mocked, tortured and finally murdered by the sons and daughters of men. We see humanity defiantly turned against God, the crea-ture, in all of its prideful arrogance, seeking to annihilate the Cre-ator. The writer of Hebrews exhorts us to "think of all the hostility he endured from sinful people" (Heb 12:3) as he endured the cross. Here our deep-seated, burning hostility toward God is fully ex-posed: *Our hatred is so intense we would kill God if we could.* In our determination to be autonomous and independent, to be our own gods, we would go so far as to get rid of God so we could take his place. Here we see not "sinners in the hands of an angry God," as Jonathan Edwards put it in his famous eighteenth-century ser-mon, but "God in the hands of angry sinners." The cross reveals how hell-bent we are and how heinous and horrible sin is.

To be sure, the Bible portrays sin in a variety of ways: falling short of God's standard, deliberately crossing a boundary, twisted-ness or perversity, weakness or infirmity. The cross, however, gets to the heart of the matter: Sin is flat-out rebellion, sheer defiance, our willful declaration of independence from God. Not merely falling short of an established standard, we would like to get rid of the One who established the standard in the first place.

Jeremiah maintained that "the human heart is the most deceitful of all things, and desperately wicked. Who really knows how bad it is?" (Jer 17:9). The cross shows us how bad! Here our true colors are exposed, our malignant nature unmasked. Theologian Alan Lewis sums it up well:

> The cross illuminates most vividly the wicked chasms of rebellion and estrangement which separate the human creatures from their Maker, the subjects from their King, by exposing so concretely the contrast between divine humility and human hubris. . . . Thus by the cross of Jesus the truth about us is smoked out; we are unmasked, denuded. Convicting truth as blasphemy, mocking the king as an imposter, delivering up to death and the Devil the Son of the living God, we are exposed as idolaters and fools, as hypocritical enemies of peace, as violent allies of the dark.[7]

How then does God respond to such deliberate, deep-seated wickedness? Does God simply ignore or excuse it? Does God say, "Listen, it doesn't matter? You would like to annihilate me. But don't worry about it, we'll just pretend it never happened." Absolutely not! The cross reveals that God takes sin much too seriously to ignore it, casually forgive it or simply speak it away. Consider what Jesus the Son—the one who, according to Paul, knew no sin but was made sin for us (2 Cor 5:21) and who, according to Peter, bore our sins in his own body on the tree (1 Pet 2:24)—experienced on the cross in his relationship to God the Father as further revelation of the seriousness of sin.

First of all, as one fully identified with sinners, Jesus experienced separation from God, as evident when he cried out in agony, quoting from Psalm 22, "My God, my God, why have you forsaken me?" (Mk 15:34 NRSV). Some maintain that this cry of dereliction was merely an expression of human emotion, a cry of a desperate man who in this extreme situation felt God-forsaken, although he actually wasn't. However, theologians over the centuries have believed that Jesus' cry was an expression of actual God-forsakenness in some sense. As he hung on the cross, the incarnate Son, who had never known a moment's separation from the Father, experienced separation from the Father. For as one fully identified with sin, he knew the separation, the alienation from God, which is an inevitable consequence of sin.

On the cross, Jesus also experienced God's wrath. Unfortunately, the wrath of God is often misconceived and misunderstood. Not some capricious, indiscriminate, irrational divine fury, it is God's pure, intense revulsion to evil in all its forms and his vigorous opposition to it. Moreover, divine wrath and divine love are often portrayed as opposites, but viewed rightly, God's wrath is an expression of God's holy love. As Miroslav Volf stresses, "God isn't wrathful in spite of being love. God is wrathful because he is love."[8]

When we paddle a canoe in the direction the stream is flowing, we experience the current as blessing, but when we paddle against the stream, we experience the same current as resistance. Similarly, we experience God's holy love as wrathful when we turn away from God and stand in opposition to him. On the cross, Jesus, as the one who became sin for us and stood in our place, felt God's vigorous opposition, God's intense revulsion of sin. He experienced the wrathful love of God.

Finally, on the cross, Jesus also experienced the judgment of God. The religious leaders had challenged him to come down from the cross (Mt 27:40-43). "Save yourself," they scoffed. "Then we'll believe you." But Jesus didn't come down or try to save himself. Jesus *died* on the cross. And by dying, Jesus experienced the judgment of God upon sin. He paid sin's wages (Rom 6:23). He tasted death and drank the cup of divine judgment. He descended to the place of the dead where all who sin are destined to go.

The cross, then, tells us just how seriously God takes our sin. God doesn't excuse it or turn and look the other way. God acknowledges it for what it is. It separates us from God, evokes divine wrath and places us under divine judgment. In an age that wants to ignore the problem of sin, deny its consequences and forget "what a heavy weight sin is," we need to preach the cross in keeping with the true nature and extreme gravity of sin.

THE COSTLINESS OF ATONEMENT

Not only does the cross graphically reveal sin, but it also reveals the incredible costliness of what God has done to atone for it. Centuries before Calvary, the prophet Isaiah foretold how God would do it: "The LORD laid on him the sins of us all" (Is 53:6). Because of his great love for us, God has chosen not to allow the punishment for our sin to fall on us, nor on some innocent third party. Rather, on the cross God chooses to let it fall on himself. As Leonard Hodson puts it, "He wills that sin shall be punished, but He does not will that sin shall be punished without also willing that the punishment shall fall upon himself."[9]

George Buttrick tells about a painting of the crucifixion that hangs in an Italian church. At first glance it looks like most other paintings of the crucifixion, but as you examine it closely you perceive that "there's a vast and shadowy Figure behind the figure of Jesus. The nail that pierces the hand of Jesus goes through to the hand of God. The spear thrust into the side of Jesus goes through into God's."[10]

The artist of that painting discerned correctly. God in the person of his Son took the consequences of our sin into himself. He endured the separation. He carried his own wrath. He bore the judgment. And at what infinite cost to himself!

Earlier I spoke of Jesus' cry of dereliction from the cross: "My God, my God, why have you forsaken me?" What he had struggled with in Gethsemane—the cup he did not want to drink that he had implored his Father to save him from—had at last come upon him. It happened on the cross. The Father, whose eyes are too pure to look on sin, forsook the Son who had become sin for us. Just as the sun was hid from view in the deep darkness at Golgotha, so he hid his face from his Son.

Centuries before, the prophet Amos had poignantly described the scene: "'In that day,' says the Sovereign LORD, 'I will make the sun go down at noon and darken the earth while it is still day. I will turn your celebrations into times of mourning . . . as if your only son had died. How very bitter that day will be!'" (Amos 8:9-10).

This, then, was the *real* cross in Jesus' crucifixion. He was forsaken by the God who he knew to be his Father, and whose Son he knew himself to be. He surrendered up his Sonship and allowed himself to become Fatherless.

But consider, too, what that meant for the Father. For if the Son loses his Sonship, that means that the Father loses his Fatherhood too. The Fatherlessness of the Son also means the Sonlessness of the Father. So in the deep darkness of Golgotha we see God forsaken by God, what Martin Luther described as "God striving with God." The love that binds the Father and the Son becomes in that moment a dividing curse. God is divided from God; God strives with God as holy love and sin meet. As a result, the infinite love of the Father for the Son is transformed into infinite pain over the sacrifice of the Son. Likewise, the infinite love of the Son for the Father turns into infinite suffering over his separation from the Father.

The cross reveals that in making atonement for sin, God doesn't ignore it, excuse it or deal with it externally. Instead God bears it himself in the person of his Son, and at such an incredible cost! As C. F. D. Moule describes it, what we see on the cross is "a radical, a drastic, a passionate and absolutely final acceptance of the terrible situation, and an absorption by the very God himself of the fatal disease so as to neutralize it effectively."[11]

But because God has dealt with it in such a substantial, costly way, a sufficient sacrifice and a full atonement has been made for sin, and a satisfactory basis for forgiveness and redemption has been firmly established. The antidote truly counteracts the effect of the deadly poison and cleanses us from the virulent infection. Because of what God has done, we can be confident that through faith in his blood, we have been forgiven, cleansed and restored to fellowship with God. Our sins, as horrible and heinous as they are, have been removed from us as far as the east is from the west (see Ps 103:12).

The cross is the clearest and profoundest revelation both of the gravity of sin and the extent to which God, in holy love, is willing to go in providing a way of atonement. As rebellious sinners, we were there at the cross, pounding in the nails, shouting, "Crucify him, crucify him!" Yet coming to terms with who we are and acknowledging what we have done is crucial if we are to grasp the depth of what, through the cross, God has done for us in Christ.

Charles Wesley captures it in his magnificent hymn "And Can It Be?": "Died he for me who caused his pain! For me, who him to death pursued?" Only when we understand this can we begin to comprehend the glory and the wonder of the cross: "Amazing love! How can it be that thou, my God, shouldst die for me?"[12]

"Were you there, when they crucified my Lord?" asks the African American spiritual. Yes, we *were* all there. "Oh! Sometimes it causes me to tremble, tremble, tremble."[13] And in the light of what we as sinners have done and what Holy Love has done in response, how can we *not* tremble?

THE CROSS AND HUMAN SUFFERING
In his seminal work *Clinical Theology,* psychiatrist and pastoral

theologian Frank Lake maintains that as fallen human beings we are all both sinners and sufferers, but as sinners and as sufferers we have two different needs. "The sinner's need is that God be reconciled to him, by forgiveness. The sufferer needs to be reconciled to God by some clear evidence that God shares his suffering and understands, by identification, what it is like. The Cross is God's supreme answer to this cry of anguish from those who suffer."[14]

Often in the past, preachers have focused so exclusively on how the cross addresses the problem of human sin that they've failed to help their hearers grasp how profoundly it addresses the problem of human suffering.[15]

For some that problem is primarily philosophical and intellectual. How can a good and righteous God allow so much suffering—particularly unjust suffering—in the world? Is a God who lets the innocent suffer and permits senseless death worthy to be called God at all? At all times and in all places, people have wrestled with these questions; yet in the world we live in today, these questions have become even more acute. Ours is a world of torture, violence, natural disasters, terrorism, genocide, famine, mass starvation, civil wars and the proliferation of nuclear weapons. It's also the world of television, the Internet and a 24/7 news cycle that constantly set these things before our eyes.

As a result, we truly have to bury our heads in the sand not to feel the force of the problem. For many unbelievers, the magnitude of unjust suffering in the world today has become the cornerstone in their wall of unbelief. But it's not only unbelievers who wrestle with this problem; many believers do too, even though they may be more hesitant to talk about it.

For others, however, the problem of suffering is more personal and experiential. It's not the unjust suffering in the world that troubles them as much as the unjust suffering they've experienced in their own lives. Deep within them there's a raging, angry voice that cries out, "God, this isn't fair! It's not right. What did I do to deserve this?"

How, then, does the cross address the problem of suffering? What is the message of the cross that we are called to proclaim for the sufferer? First of all, the cross tells us in no uncertain terms that God in Christ is one with us in our suffering. The prophet Isaiah, in describing the future servant Messiah, calls him "a man of sorrows, acquainted with deepest grief" (Is 53:3), someone who would know pain and suffering firsthand. When we suffer then, God doesn't stand far off, aloof, unable or unwilling to get involved. Jesus is Emmanuel, God with us, who, as we saw in the last chapter, identifies fully with the human condition. At the cross, particularly in relation to human suffering, the meaning of Emmanuel is fully and finally disclosed.

There he personally experienced human suffering in all its ranges. As Lake maintains, the events surrounding the cross "portray every variety of human suffering and evil"[16] He points out that on the cross Jesus suffered injustice, felt the shame of nakedness, was deprived of his rights, endured taunting, became the focus of the rage of others, and was rejected and forsaken. In addition, he experienced excruciating physical pain, thirst, hunger, emptiness, torment, confusion and finally even death itself.

Having personally experienced such breadth and depth of human suffering, Jesus can truly identify with us when we suffer. He is, in A. N. Whitehead's phrase, "the fellow sufferer who understands." Because Christ "learned obedience from the things he suffered" (Heb 5:8), he can empathetically identify with us in our anguish.

A university student whom Frank Lake had been counseling wrote to him of how this finally dawned on her. Late one night, she was sitting alone in a chapel, railing at God for allowing so much pain and suffering in her life and the lives of others:

I was livid with His apathy. Didn't He *know* what His care-
lessness had done to us? For the first time in my life I dared
to demand an explanation. When none came, I was angrier
than I ever remember being. I turned my eyes on to the
plain wooden cross and I remembered Calvary. I stood in
the crowd which crucified him, hating and despising him.
With my own hands I drove the nails into his hands and
his feet, and with bursting energy I flogged him and reviled
him and spat with nauseated loathing. Now *He* should
know what it felt like—to live in the creation He had made.
Every breath brought from me the words: "Now You know!
Now You know!"

And then I saw something which made my heart stand
still. I saw His face, and on it twisted every familiar agony of
my own soul. "Now You know" became an awed whisper as
I, motionless, watched His agony. "Yes, now I know" was the
passionate and pain-filled reply. "Why else should I come?"
Stunned, I watched His eyes search desperately for the tini-
est flicker of love in mine, and as we faced one another in the
bleak and the cold, forsaken by God, frightened and derelict,
we loved one another and our pain became silent in the
calm.

Nothing can bind us closer than common dereliction for
nowhere else is companionship so longed for.[17]

From that moment she was inseparably bound to Christ. No
matter how difficult the path toward healing, no matter how
strange and perilous the steps he was inviting her to take seemed,
she clung tightly to this One who knew. Even when she couldn't
trace his hand, she knew she could trust his heart. Knowing that
Jesus became a man of sorrows and had experienced dereliction
like hers was enough.

That is the first part of the message of the cross we need to proclaim to a suffering world and to hurting people. It doesn't make our own personal suffering disappear, nor does it solve the age-old enigma of suffering, but it does enable us to keep trusting God even in the presence of the inexplicable. No matter what happens, nothing can separate us from his love. John Stott's words in *The Cross of Christ* get to the heart of it:

> I could never myself believe in God if it were not for the cross. . . . In the real world of pain, how could one worship a God who was immune to it? [At the cross] He laid aside his immunity to pain. He entered our world of flesh and blood, tears and death. He suffered for us. Our sufferings become more manageable in the light of his. There is still a question mark against human suffering, but over it we boldly stamp another mark, the cross which symbolizes divine suffering. [As P. T. Forsyth wrote,] "The cross of Christ . . . is God's only self-justification in such a world as ours."[18]

But not only does the cross tell us that God is one with us in our suffering, it also tells us that God uses suffering in redeeming his fallen creation. God's solution to the problem of suffering is not to eliminate it, nor to insulate himself from it, but to participate in it, and having participated in it, to transform it into his instrument for redeeming the world.

The cross tells us that God can use suffering. We must proclaim that too. God weaves it into his redemptive plan and pattern for the salvation of the world and for our salvation too. He takes the terrible tragedy of the cross and turns it into a triumph. What is grotesque becomes glorious, what is evil is transmuted into what is good.

Emil Brunner is right: "If there ever were an event in which evil, innocent suffering, malice and human pain reaches its climax, it is in the cross of Christ."[19] Yet God took all the awful elements of that event—the diabolical evil, the flagrant injustice, the excruciating pain—mixed them all together, and through his marvelous divine alchemy transformed them into his divine medicine for the healing of the nations.

The cross, then, is the supreme illustration of Romans 8:28, "that God causes everything to work together for the good of those who love God and are called according to his purpose for them." It proves that even when things seem to have gone tragically wrong, God can still use anguish creatively to bring out of it blessings that could not have been realized any other way. In fact, this is God's method: this is how God, in the face of evil, works to accomplish his will and his purpose in the world.

How does God overcome that which opposes his will? How does God demonstrate his sovereignty and power in the face of evil? The cross proclaims that it is through a power that absorbs the opposition to his will through innocent suffering. Then having absorbed it, God neutralizes it by forgiving love. And finally, having neutralized evil, God uses it to accomplish the very purpose it was originally trying to thwart.

Through the cross, God overcomes evil, not through brute strength, not through coercion or manipulation, not through a dazzling display of force, but through the power of suffering love. God uses suffering redemptively to accomplish his will and his purpose in the world and in our lives.

In her book *Blessings*, Mary Craig writes about how she came to realize this. Two of her four sons were born with severe abnormalities. Caring for them was difficult and resulted in an intense spiritual struggle for her. But in the last chapter, as she reflects on the meaning of suffering, she speaks about its "redemptive power." "In the teeth of the evidence I do not believe that any suffering is ultimately absurd or pointless," even though "it is often difficult to go on convincing oneself" of this. When suffering comes, we usually react in disbelief, anger or despair. But, "the value of suffering does not lie in the pain of it . . . but in what the sufferer makes of it. . . . It is in sorrow that we discover the things which really matter; in sorrow that we discover ourselves."[20]

The cross, then, speaks volumes to us about the problem of human suffering. It tells us, in no uncertain terms, that God is one with us in our suffering. It demonstrates that God can use suffering redemptively in accomplishing his purposes for us. There will always be those in our congregations wrestling with issues related to past or present suffering in their lives. Others will be struggling to understand the extent of unjust suffering and tragedy in our fallen world. How lovely, then, are the feet of those preachers who proclaim this good news (Is 52:7; Rom 10:15), this message of the cross for the sufferer.

THE CROSS AS THE SUPREME REVELATION OF GOD'S LOVE

"God is love" (1 Jn 4:8)—we have heard it quoted so often that for Christians it has become an axiomatic unquestioned belief, along with "God so loved the world" (Jn 3:16). If there is a God, how can that God not be love?

Yet when John first penned those words, the conviction that God is love was far from self-evident. In fact, the pre-Christian and non-Christian religions of his day had deified every quality *except* self-giving love. The only deity missing from the world's pantheon was the God who is love.

As Christians we tend to take it for granted. Doesn't everybody know that God is love? Yet what was true in John's day still stands: no other major religion in the world proclaims that God *is* love. In Islam, for example, Allah can choose to *act* lovingly, but it is not what Allah *is*. Love is not his essential nature. Only the Christian religion makes such a bold, audacious claim.

What's more, it stakes that claim on an historical event: Christ's death on the cross. This is how we know that God is love, says John, "not that we loved God, but that he loved us and *sent his Son as a sacrifice to take away our sins*" (1 Jn 4:10, italics mine). In the apostle's mind, the two are inextricably bound up together: the love of God and Christ's death on the cross. In fact, if you dispense with the one (Christ's death) you lose the other (God's love). As Robert Law clearly demonstrates in his classic study of 1 John, "the conviction, the idea that God is Love, has been generated by nothing else than belief in Jesus Christ as Incarnate God Who laid down His life for man's redemption."[21]

In our preaching, then, we must proclaim the close connection between the cross and the love of God. In a world of inexplicable evil, suffering and tragedy that often calls divine love into question, our best response is to point to the cross and say, "There on a day in history, on a hill outside the city of Jerusalem, the incarnate Son of God was crucified for us. That's how we know with certainty that God is love." In the words of the great hymn that was written and became the theme song during the Welsh revival:

> Here is love, vast as the ocean,
> Loving-kindness as the flood;
> When the Prince of Life, my ransom,
> Shed for me his precious blood.
> Who his love will not remember?
> Who can cease to sing his praise?
> He shall never be forgotten,
> Through heav'n's everlasting days.[22]

While the cross is the supreme evidence that God is love, it is also the clearest revelation of the nature of divine love. God is love, yes, and the cross is the proof or demonstration of it (Rom 5:8), but what kind of love is it? The cross also reveals that. There is much to proclaim here, but let's consider just three characteristics of God's love.

The cross tells of the extensive nature of God's love. Paul underscores this when he states that "God showed his great love for us by sending Christ to die for us *while we were still sinners"* (Rom 5:8, italics mine). It wasn't while we were at our religious best, sincerely seeking after God, that Christ died for us. But while we were sinners who were, as we've described above, sworn enemies of God, out-and-out rebels, defiant creatures hell-bent on annihilating our Creator, he died for us.

While we were at our absolute worst, then, God loved us the most. That's how extensive God's love is for us. The cross proves that no one, no matter how wicked, depraved and reprobate they are, is beyond the scope of Calvary's love. Christ died for us all because God's love extends to all.

In an interview with a journalist following the failure of her marriage to the Prince of Wales, Princess Diana sadly commented, "The greatest disease in the world is the disease of being unloved."[23] The cross proves that is a disease from which no one needs to suffer. Christ's arms on the cross, open and outstretched, point to the extensive nature of God's love. No one is beyond its reach.

The cross tells of the expensive nature of God's love. Our understanding of the love of God can very easily degenerate into sentimentalism or what someone has aptly termed "sloppy agape." In an age that prizes tolerance to a fault, it is easy to project our extreme understandings of tolerance onto God. We therefore assume that a God of love will tolerate sin and forgive it without difficulty or cost.

As we have seen, however, God's love is not a sentimental, but an intensely *holy* love. God does not glibly tolerate or casually ignore the rupture in the divine-human relationship caused by sin, but he deals with our sinful rebellion and wicked defiance with utmost seriousness. Forgiveness is free, but it is certainly not cheap.

The words of John quoted above, which stressed that the cross is the supreme proof that God is love, also underscore the costly nature of that love. God "loved us," he says, "and sent his Son as a sacrifice to take away our sins" (1 Jn 4:10). The Greek word *hilasterion,* translated here as "sacrifice" and in other versions as "atoning sacrifice," "propitiation" or "expiation," is drawn from the Old Testament sacrificial system. New Testament scholars and theologians continue to debate about its precise meaning. Does it have to do with averting divine wrath (propitiation) or annulling human guilt (expiation), or is it a combination of both?[24] We are not going to try to resolve that debate here. Suffice it to say that this word, given its close association with sacrifice, certainly underscores the costliness of divine love. In making atonement for sin, God does not look the other way or sidestep holiness. But in holy love, God himself, as he did with Abraham on Mount Moriah (Gen 22:8), provides the sacrificial lamb. Indeed, God will sacrifice himself in the person of his Son.

In analyzing Paul's linking of the cross and the love of God, New Testament scholar Michael Gorman delineates three characteristics of what he calls "cruciform love."[25] All of them serve to underscore the costly nature of divine love. First, it is *sacrificial love* in that it is on behalf of others. Whenever Paul uses phrases like "Christ Jesus died for us" (Rom 8:34) or "Christ died for all" (2 Cor 5:14), according to Gorman he is depicting the costliness of Christ's action for others. Second, it is a *self-giving love.* Paul uses reflexive phrases, like he "gave himself for me" (Gal 2:20), he "made himself nothing" (Phil 2:7 NIV) and he "humbled himself in obedience" (Phil 2:8), to make this point. Third, it is a *status-renouncing love.* When Paul contrasts the Son of God's preexistent form of existence with his incarnate form of existence—such as in 2 Corinthians 8:9, or in Philippians 2:6-8 and Romans 15:3—he is describing this dimension of love. Here Paul emphasizes how Christ deliberately and freely chose to abandon his status so that he could give himself for others. God's love, then, revealed on the cross, is not only an *expansive* but an *expensive* love.

The cross tells of the exemplary nature of God's love. The New Testament writers stress this third characteristic of God's love: "Since God loved us that much," says John in reference to the love demonstrated on the cross, "we surely ought to love each other" (1 Jn 4:11). The love revealed at the cross provides the example, the pattern and the impetus for our loving others. That's why Paul, likewise, urges the Ephesians, "Live a life filled with love, following the example of Christ. He loved us and offered himself as a sacrifice for us" (Eph 5:2).

First and foremost that includes those who are our brothers and sisters in Christ in the Christian community, the church. So Paul, having urged Philippian believers to "make [him] truly happy by agreeing wholeheartedly with each other, loving one another, and working together with one heart and purpose" (Phil 2:2), proceeds to remind them of Christ's example, who "made himself nothing" and who "humbled himself even further by dying a criminal's death on a cross" (Phil 2:7-8). But such love must also extend to those outside the household of faith, even to those who are persecuting us for our faith. As Peter exhorts his fellow Christians, many of whom were being mistreated on account of their faith, "Christ, who suffered for you, is your example. Follow in his steps" (1 Pet 2:21).

We must preach the cross not only as a demonstration of divine love, but as the pattern and example for us. It not only tells us what God's love looks like, but it also tells us what *our* love should look like. His cruciform love was sacrificial, self-giving and status-renouncing. So must ours be. "Love so amazing, so divine, demands my soul, my life, my all."[26]

4

PREACHING THE CROSS

SOCIAL EVIL, VICTORY, DYING WITH CHRIST

As he was suspended there, bound hand and foot to the wood
in apparent weakness, they imagined they had him in their grasp,
and flung themselves on him with hostile intent.
But, far from suffering their attack without resistance,
he grappled with them and mastered them,
stripping them of all the armor in which they trusted,
and held them aloft in his mighty outstretched hands,
displaying to the universe their helplessness
and his own unvanquished strength.

F. F. BRUCE

Truly, the cross is a many-splendored thing, a many-faceted diamond. We must preach it in its various dimensions to demonstrate how wonderfully sufficient it is in meeting our need for redemption and restoration. In the last chapter we addressed four such facets or dimensions—scandal, atonement, suffering and love—and now we'll move on to consider three more.

THE CROSS AND SOCIAL EVIL
In the last hundred years Christians have become increasingly

aware of social dimensions of sin and evil. Of course, sin is personal, involving the actions and attitudes of particular individuals. But sin is also social, involving the actions and attitudes of collective groups of people, becoming enmeshed in systems, manifesting itself in impersonal, cultural, political, economic, intellectual and religious forces as well.

One reason the social character of sin has been neglected in the past is because sin in this form is harder to confront than personal sin. How do you pin it down or know who's actually responsible for it? There was a sharecropper during the Depression who went to the bank to find out who had made the decision to foreclose on his farm. It wasn't the local banker—he told the sharecropper he was responsible to the home office. But neither was it the home office—it was responsible to the board of directors. Nor was it the board of directors—they were obliged to the thousands of stockholders.

So what did the sharecropper conclude? That nobody was guilty because everybody was guilty. The whole system was guilty. But how do you confront a system that seems to have a life of its own and is bigger than the sum of its parts?

A former president of Midas Muffler Corporation described high-level executives in the corporate world like this: "They are strapped, rigidly and cruelly constrained to their functions as head of corporations, and secretly they are barely hanging on to a position in which they alone hope that no one will discover that no one pays very much attention to them after all." Corporations, he went on to say, are "a circumstance of large, impersonal forces over which no one seems to have much control."[1]

How then do you confront sin in this form? How do you get ahold of something you can't get your hands on? Moreover, when you do confront social evil by devising solutions for its problems, often the solutions end up creating other problems. For example, welfare payments, given to sustain life, end up breeding dependency, which stifles initiative. The arms race, supposedly begun to preserve peace, leads to unavoidable and meaningless wars. Trade policies designed to protect workers in industrial nations hurt workers in developing nations. Material problems solved by technology and growth deplete natural resources and threaten the ecological balance.

Truly, we are enmeshed in social and structural evil, but how do we break free? And just when we think we have, it pops up somewhere else.

According to the New Testament, one of the reasons evil in this form is so difficult to deal with is because it stems not merely from human beings or social forces, but from supernatural spiritual beings and forces as well. Behind the persons and the systems are principalities and powers, world rulers of this present darkness, and spiritual hosts of wickedness in the heavenly places (Rom 8:38; 1 Cor 2:6, 8; 15:24; Eph 1:21; 3:10; 6:12; Col 1:16; 2:10, 15).

These "principalities and powers," as they are most often called, are supernatural spiritual beings created by God, but like Satan they have turned against God. Having joined Satan in his rebellion, they now act as his subordinates, working to promote evil in various arenas including the social, structural realm.[2]

Like the principalities and powers themselves, the various social systems and structures—political, social, cultural, economic, intellectual and religious—were originally created by God to serve humanity. Remove them and there would be chaos in human society. We can't live without them.

However, through the seductive influence of the principalities and powers, these structures have fallen. Now instead of serving humanity, they insist on being served. Claiming to be absolute, they demand that we bow down and worship them. As a result, they dehumanize and enslave. We can't live with them!

How, then, do we preach the cross in relation to this important issue? How does the cross address the problem of social evil and the spiritual forces behind it?

We can begin by drawing attention to the social forms of evil that played a part in Christ's crucifixion. After all, it wasn't primarily an individual or even a group of individuals who crucified Jesus. A much larger coalition of religious and political and public forces were at work.

Institutional religion played a part in Jesus' crucifixion. All of them—the high priest, the chief priests, the scribes and the elders—the whole Sanhedrin tried him and condemned him to death. Then they used their collective influence and power in pressuring Pilate to crucify him.

Why was this Galilean preacher such a threat to them anyway? One of the charges they brought against him is revealing: "This man said, 'I am able to destroy the Temple of God and rebuild it in three days'" (Mt 26:61). God had given them the temple and the law so they could properly worship him, but through the influence of the principalities and powers, they were now worshiping these things, finding their identity and security in them instead of God. Jesus was a threat to them because he called into question their objects of worship. That's why they were determined to kill him.

Government and politics also played a part in Jesus' death. Pilate acted on behalf of the Roman Empire in sentencing Jesus to death as did the soldiers who drove the nails into his hands and feet. But why did Pilate do it? He knew Jesus was innocent, so what finally persuaded him to crucify Jesus? According to John's account, it was when the Jewish leaders shouted, "If you release this man, you are no 'friend of Caesar.' Anyone who declares himself a king is a rebel against Caesar" (Jn 19:12).

Caesar, the state, is ordained by God (Rom 13:1), but under the influence of the principalities and powers, it too always ends up absolutising itself, demanding worship and total allegiance. Pilate was a slave to it; Jesus was a victim of it—a victim of crucifixion, a form of institutionalized violence used by the Romans to demonstrate and preserve the absoluteness of the state.

And of course, public opinion played its part in Jesus' death too. Collectively the common people exerted a powerful influence, and the Jewish leaders knew how important the will of the people was in pressuring Pilate. So they manipulated the crowd, and their unscrupulous tactics worked. The fickle crowd gave in to pressure, expediency, apathy and self-preservation. Palm Sunday's "Hosanna! Hosanna!" quickly turned into Good Friday's "Crucify! Crucify!"

PRINCIPALITIES AND POWERS

When we consider what crucified Jesus, we have to take these larger corporate forces into account. And even more importantly, we have to take the forces behind these forces, the principalities and powers, into account. David Buttrick sums it up well, "Yes, human beings acted to crucify Christ, but they did so within collectivities, swayed by forms of social ideology. . . . The only way to make sense of crucifixion is to see the principalities and powers converging on Calvary."[3] At the cross Jesus felt the full force and fury of their attack.

But it was precisely here, at the very depth of his exposure and weakness, that Jesus, in conquering the principalities and powers, demonstrated the height of his glory and power. As Paul declares, "And having disarmed the powers and authorities, he made a public spectacle of them, triumphing over them by the cross" (Col 2:15 NIV).

Notice the three verbs Paul uses to describe how Christ won the victory over the powers. First, he "disarmed" them by taking their weapons right out of their hands. The great weapon of the principalities and powers is the power of illusion. They use it to delude us into believing that they're absolute, ultimate and worthy of worship.

Jesus, however, refused to become a slave to their illusion. He was a willing subject of the Roman and Jewish political and religious structures of his day. But he was never under any illusion concerning their authority and was unwilling to bow down and worship them. That's why they had to kill him—because they couldn't own him. Yet by voluntarily laying his life down, he proved their claim to have power over life and death was false. And by being obedient even to the point of death (Phil 2:8), he demonstrated, once and for all, he wasn't their slave and was free from their illusion.

Second, Jesus "made a public spectacle of them." The chief priests and scribes claimed to be representatives of God. Pilate and the Roman authorities claimed that God had appointed them to rule. But when confronted with God himself in the person of his Son, they wouldn't acknowledge and worship him. "If they had, they would not have crucified our glorious Lord," Paul reminds the Corinthians (1 Cor 2:8).

But they *did* crucify him, and in doing so, they revealed their true colors, exposed their real nature. They claimed to be God's agents, but in reality they were God's adversaries, agents of false gods, the principalities and powers.

Third, as a result of disarming and exposing them, on the cross Christ "triumphed" over the principalities and powers. He did this not by beating them at their own game in resorting to brute force or a stunning display of power, but by obedience, forgiveness, meekness and the power of suffering love. As Peter reminded early Christians who were being persecuted, "He did not retaliate when he was insulted, nor threaten revenge when he suffered" (1 Pet 2:23). And because he remained free, uncontaminated and uncompromised, the powers could gain no hold on him and had to concede defeat. Derek Tidball sums it up well: "Having done their worst, they overreached themselves. Having played their trump card, they were trumped. The cross means that the enemies have been outwitted and conquered."[4]

CONFRONTING THE PRINCIPALITIES AND POWERS

Yet when we consider the world we live in today, social, systemic evil is still present all around us, and the principalities and powers are still hard at work. How do we account for that in the light of their defeat on the cross? Given the pervasiveness of social evil today, we could easily conclude that the victory Christ won there has really made no difference at all.

To rightly understand the nature of Christ's victory over the powers, we must remember that we live in the tension between the *already*—what God has accomplished through the life, death, resurrection and ascension of Christ—and the *not yet*—what God will accomplish when Christ returns in glory. Christ, on the cross, has *already* decisively defeated the principalities and powers, but they have *not yet* conceded defeat, though one day they will. In fact, because their time is running out, they are redoubling their efforts and working overtime. Keeping that in mind, how should Christ's decisive victory over the principalities and powers shape our approach to them in the *already/not yet* age in which we live?

First, it should create in us a *confidence*, reflected in a cheerful impudence, when we encounter the principalities and powers. We should be like the early Christians. Because they knew that Jesus had triumphed over the principalities and powers on the cross, they knew that the world powers were nothing more than false powers, pseudo powers. That's why they were unimpressed by Caesar's armies, pagan temples or the aggregate wealth of the ancient world.

Remember the story of the emperor's new clothes and what the brash little boy said when the emperor strutted by in what was supposedly a beautiful new robe? "He's naaaked!" The early Christians were bold and impudent like that. They looked at the powers of the ancient world, and they chuckled, "No power at all. They're naaaked!"

Knowing what Jesus accomplished on the cross, we too must be confident. In our preaching we must demote the powers and expose their nakedness to the world.

Second, Christ's triumph over the powers ought to lead to *concern* on our part. Have Christians today—the church—been seduced by the powers? Have we bought into their value system? Have we become overly impressed with and enamored of wealth, prestige, size, social prominence and political clout? For these are not the values of Christ, but of anti-Christ, of the principalities and powers. Such concern should cause us to humble ourselves, to examine ourselves, to "keep watch and pray" so that we won't be overpowered by temptation (Mt 26:41).

Third, confidence and concern should lead to *concentration*. In Ephesians 3:10 Paul states that through the church God purposes "to display his wisdom in its rich variety to all the unseen rulers and authorities in the heavenly places." In the church, God has brought into being a new community and established a new social order that lives according to the values of its crucified and risen Lord Jesus Christ. So by its very existence, the church witnesses to the fact that Jesus is Lord and he has disarmed and defeated the principalities and powers.

The most important thing the church can do, then, is to simply be the church, to truly live as a distinctive, salt-and-light community (Mt 5:13-16) under the lordship of Christ, according to his purposes and design, without allowing itself to be seduced by the values of the principalities and powers. That should always be the church's primary social strategy. Above all, the church should concentrate on being the church.

Fourth, in addition to this primary social strategy, there is a secondary strategy that is important as well: *confronting* unjust social systems, speaking out on behalf of those who are oppressed by them, promoting peace and justice in the world, working to bring the laws of society in conformity with the laws of Christ. That's why a Christian leader like John Wesley in eighteenth-century England worked primarily to evangelize unbelievers and establish Christian communities where believers could be nurtured, discipled and held accountable. But he also wrote pamphlets against smuggling, bribery at elections and intemperance; admonished the government to do something about high unemployment and the cost of food; supported the campaign against slavery; and opened medical dispensaries, schools, orphanages and homes for aged widows.

When we are engaged in such activities, we confront the principalities and powers and witness to the world that Jesus is Lord. As Paul Fiddes explains, "If we hold a world view in which the powers have been placed under the Lordship of Christ, then we have a right to resist powers when they are in rebellion against the divine intention for human life."[5]

Confidence, concern, concentration, confrontation—preaching this fourfold approach to the principalities and powers will certainly be challenging. Social issues are often complex, so we must avoid simplistic solutions and gross generalizations. Our preaching must be clear, and we must carefully explain what we mean. Moreover, since many in our congregations have never heard preaching relating the cross to social evil, it may strike them as strange and foreign to the gospel. Some will find it offensive, unpatriotic, perhaps even unbiblical.

Preaching, then, on such issues will take courage, for it is sure to provoke controversy and misunderstanding. Challenging the status quo won't win us any popularity contests. But how can we be faithful to the gospel and *not* preach about such issues to which the cross speaks so pertinently and powerfully? Preach, then, on the social dimensions of the cross.

THE CROSS AS CHRIST'S VICTORY OVER SATAN
In *God's Word in Man's Language,* published in 1952, Eugene Nida, the famous Bible translator, tells of a conversation between a mis-

sionary and a West African who was helping translate the Scripture into the Bambara language. "How would you say 'God redeemed us' so that your own Bambara people will understand?" the missionary inquired.

"You should say, 'God took our heads out,'" was the strange reply. The missionary was puzzled. *How will they understand that?* he wondered.

"Years ago Arab slave traders would make raids upon our people," the African explained. "They would capture them, put an iron collar around their necks and chain them to one another. Then they would form them in long lines and drive them to the coast.

"Sometimes, however, when they were passing near a village, a local chief might see friends or relatives being led away into slavery and would work to have them freed. So he would barter with the slave traders, and if he paid them enough gold or silver or ivory, his friends or relatives would be set free and, literally, their heads would be taken out of the iron collar."

So today, says Nida, Bambara preachers, in telling the story of God's redeeming love, explain to their people that "God saw us in slavery to sin and self, being driven under the lash of Satan, and so He sent His Son to die that [we] might live. Thus He redeemed us, literally, 'He took our heads out.' 'And furthermore,' they explain, 'just as in ancient times a redeemed slave felt an obligation to serve for a lifetime the one who had thus redeemed him, so we may be the voluntary slaves of Jesus Christ.'"[6]

Of course in declaring that Jesus' death redeems us and sets us free from slavery to sin and self and Satan, Bambara preachers today are underscoring a prominent element in the New Testament message of the cross—one that we should proclaim too. In fact, during the apostolic era and continuing for the first thousand years of church history, it was the primary way Christian preachers and theologians explained the significance of the death of

Jesus. Through his death, they insisted, Christ won a great victory over Satan and has set us free from his enslaving power.

To be sure, throughout his ministry Jesus was engaged in warfare and combat with Satan. Every time he healed the sick, cast out demons, fed the hungry or stilled a storm, he was winning a battle in the war against the evil one. But there was a final, climactic battle, a turning point in the war where he inflicted a mortal wound on his archenemy. That battle was fought and won on the cross, where he fought the devil in the realm of death. As the writer of Hebrews declares, "Only by dying could he break the power of the devil, who had the power of death. Only in this way could he set free all who have lived their lives as slaves to the fear of dying" (Heb 2:14-15).

At the cross, Jesus, the mighty dragon slayer, went into the dragon's den—where he exercised his greatest power, the power of death—to slay the dragon. There he stormed the gates of hell, trampling underfoot the powers of darkness. There he crushed the head of the serpent (Gen 3:15), wounding him with a fatal blow. There as a conqueror he shouted triumphantly, "It is finished" (Jn 19:30). Now the back of Satan's neck is engraved with a nail-scarred footprint!

However, as we've already emphasized, Christ waged the battle on the cross not with brute strength, by overcoming power with power, or through a direct violent frontal attack on Satan. As Augustine and other church fathers often stressed, Christ overcame the devil "not by power but by justice."[7]

What they meant is clearly spelled out in Colossians 2:13-15. We have already discussed the three verbs Paul uses in verse 15 to vividly portray Christ's victory on the cross over the principalities and powers (he disarmed, exposed and triumphed over them). Now consider the immediately preceding three verbs in verse 14 to explain how he won it. He *canceled* the record that contained the charges against us, *set it aside* and *nailed it* to the cross. The *cheirographon,* the legal record with all of its demands, our great IOU for sin, the huge debt that we can never repay—Jesus paid it on the cross and stamped "Paid in Full" on the record that stood against us. And by removing that record he took away the devil's legal claim on us.

That's how he won his climactic battle with Satan. Not by some direct, blitzkrieg show of force, but by removing the devil's right to hold us in his power. By liberating us from sin, he therefore liberated us from Satan.

In *The Lion, the Witch and the Wardrobe,* C. S. Lewis artfully shapes the story to make the same point. By betraying Peter, Susan and Lucy for the Turkish delight offered him, Edmund becomes a prisoner and slave of the White Witch. Later he is rescued by Aslan's forces and brought to Aslan's camp, where he is reunited with his brother and sisters. When he meets the Lion-king, he expresses his sorrow for what he has done.

But then the White Witch herself marches into Aslan's camp, demanding that Edmund be returned to her. Because of the Deep Magic written into Narnia from the dawn of time, she insists she still has legal rights over Edmund: "For every traitor belongs to me as my lawful prey and for every treachery I have a right to a kill. . . . And so, that human creature is mine. His life is forfeit to me. His blood is my property."[8]

One of Aslan's soldiers challenges her to enforce her claim. Who cares about her so-called legal rights? Edmund is with Aslan now, and she knows she's no match for him. He would never let her lay a finger on Edmund. But the witch sneers back, "Fool, . . . do you really think your master can rob me of my rights by mere force? He knows the Deep Magic better than that. He knows that unless I have blood as the Law says all Narnia will be overturned and perish in fire and water."[9]

To everyone's surprise, Aslan doesn't dispute what she says. He speaks with her privately, and they come to an agreement that he will take Edmund's place. His blood will be given in exchange for Edmund's. That night, Aslan enters the enemy camp and turns himself over to her. His feet are bound and his mane is shaved before the knife is thrust into his heart. Aslan is killed on the large altar-like stone table.

Of course, that's not the end of the story. Aslan miraculously comes back to life; there is a joyous reunion and victory romp with Susan and Lucy. But then they want to know what it all means. And what about the Deep Magic? Aslan explains that the witch's knowledge of the Deep Magic only went back to the creation of Narnia. It didn't go back far enough—to before the dawn of time. If it had, "she would have known that when a willing victim who had committed no treachery was killed in a traitor's stead, the Table would crack and death itself would start working backwards."[10]

The witch later meets her end in a final battle with Aslan, the children and the talking animals. But notice that as Jesus did on the cross, Aslan defeats the witch on the stone table in Narnia not by power but by justice.

We must be clear, then, in proclaiming that Christ won the victory not by sheer might but by the power of suffering love. But we must also trumpet the victory itself and the freedom Christ has won for us. Because of what he accomplished on the cross, he truly can "take our heads out." He can set us free from our bondage to Satan and all his works. That, according to John the apostle, is the reason the Son of God came: "to destroy the works of the devil" (1 Jn 3:8).

What exactly are the works of the devil? According to John Stott, the New Testament writers concentrate on four: the law, the flesh (fallen human nature), the world (godless society) and death.[11] Moreover, "destroying them" doesn't mean they're completely obliterated and cease to exist, but that their power has been broken. "They have not been abolished," Stott explains, "but they have been overthrown."[12]

These are important caveats in helping people understand the already/not yet victory of Christ they can experience in their lives. But proclaim it we must. Christ won a victory on the cross over Satan and all his works. Therefore there is release for the captives and deliverance for those who are bound.

A missionary nurse told John Taylor, an Anglican bishop, an amazing story of an unlikely proclaimer of that good news and its life-changing effects.[13] In the late 1960s, she was serving in a hospital established by the Anglican church in Peshawar, a remote city in western Pakistan on the edge of the Khyber pass.

An English hippie named Dick wandered into that hospital one day, terribly sick. He was a heroin addict, and since heroin was plentiful and cheap in that region, he had been living there for several months. Besides being an addict, he had hepatitis and venereal disease. He responded positively to treatment, but refused to stay in the hospital because he craved drugs too much. So before he was completely well, he left to wander about.

However, it wasn't long before his health deteriorated again, and one day when he was roaming the countryside, he fell unconscious and was found lying on a hillside by an older man named Ahmed. Ahmed was a fierce, rugged Baluchi tribesman. He was a devout Muslim, and his religion dictated that he show mercy and compassion on strangers and foreigners. So he picked Dick up, carried him to his own village and began to nurse him back to health again. But Dick was still an addict, and Ahmed knew that Dick couldn't live without his drugs, so for a while he supplied him with heroin.

One day, however, after Dick's health had significantly improved, Ahmed began to talk straight to him about his heroin addiction. Because he had served in the British army years before, Ahmed could speak broken English. "There's only one hope for you," he insisted. "Dick, you must pray and ask God to deliver you from your addiction. But when you pray, don't pray to Allah, pray to *Isa*, pray to Messiah Jesus. He's the one who can heal you and set you free."

In his desperation, Dick took Ahmed's advice to heart. He began to cry out to Jesus and was miraculously delivered and set free. Not long afterward, he went back to the hospital for further treatment, and the nurse, who had worked with him before, couldn't get over the dramatic change in him. Now he was a polite, cooperative patient, and he kept talking about the Lord Jesus, the one who had set him free.

One day she said to him, "How in the world did this happen to you? And who out here told you about Jesus?" When he told her it was a Baluchi tribesman named Ahmed who lived in a certain village, she couldn't believe it—she knew Ahmed herself and what a fiercely devout Muslim he was. *Why would he tell someone about Jesus?* she wondered. Yet Dick kept insisting that he had.

Several months later, after Dick had left the hospital and the area and returned home to England, Ahmed showed up at the hospital for some outpatient treatment. While he was there, this same nurse asked him if what Dick had said was true. "Ahmed," she inquired, "did you tell Dick, that man you found with the heroin addiction, to pray to Jesus?"

"Oh, yes, Madam," Ahmed replied, "I certainly did."

"But Ahmed, why? Are you a Christian now?"

Ahmed was incensed. "Oh, no, Madam! Allah is my God and Muhammad is my prophet."

"So why, Ahmed? Why did you tell him to pray to Jesus?"

Then Ahmed explained, "Oh, Madam, for ordinary people and in ordinary situations you should pray to Allah. But in cases like this one where there is really no hope and where the power of Sythan (Satan) has complete hold of a person, then there is only one name to pray to: *Isa* (Jesus). Only *Isa* (Jesus) can save us from Sythan's power. This I firmly believe."

How true! And how amazing! An old devout Muslim, in the

frontier land of the Khyber, preaches to a lost and enslaved English hippie the message of freedom in Christ, all made possible through his victory won on the cross. We must preach it too: there is freedom and deliverance for those who are bound. Like Dick, we can be set free from bondages and addictions. Jesus can save us from Satan's power. Through his cross he can deliver us from all the works of the devil.

CRUCIFIED WITH CHRIST

Up to now, in considering various ways of proclaiming the significance of the cross of Christ, we have been viewing it primarily as a past event—the most decisive event in history, no doubt, and one that has profound implications for us today, but nevertheless, an event in the past. Yet according to the New Testament writers, the cross is to be seen not only as a past event, but also as a present experience in the life of every Christian. As Derek Tidball explains, "Using language that is nothing short of astonishing, disciples of Christ are called upon not only to derive the benefits from his historic crucifixion, but to crucify themselves daily. The Christian life paradoxically means dying with Christ. The believer's lot is to live a cruciform way of life."[14]

In *Cruciformity,* New Testament scholar Michael Gorman shows how crucial it was to the apostle Paul that his own life told the same story of the cross he was preaching. "His spirituality," he observes, "was therefore a *narrative spirituality,* an experience of re-presenting in living form the word of the cross."[15]

Preachers have often proclaimed the benefits of Christ's historical death on the cross without proclaiming the necessity of the cross in the present experience of the Christian. The result is what Dietrich Bonhoeffer aptly called "cheap grace," that is, "grace without discipleship, grace without the cross, grace without Jesus Christ, living and incarnate."[16] His *The Cost of Discipleship* was written to counteract this deadly enemy of the church. Participating in and carrying the cross is not optional for the Christian, Bonhoeffer declares, but is inherent in Christian discipleship:

> The cross is laid on every Christian. . . . As we embark upon discipleship we surrender ourselves to Christ in union with his death—we give over our lives to death. Thus it begins; the cross is not the terrible end to an otherwise god-fearing and happy life, but it meets us at the beginning of our communion with Christ. When Christ calls a man, he bids him come and die.[17]

As Jesus himself said, "If any of you wants to be my follower, you must turn from your selfish ways, take up your cross, and follow me" (Mk 8:34). To be true to the message of the cross, the cross in the life of the disciple must be taken into account. And based on the New Testament, particularly the writings of Paul, the disciple's cross has several different dimensions that need to be included in our preaching.

First, there is the cross of *identification*, which has to do with our initial union with Christ, our laying hold of the benefits of Christ's death and resurrection through justifying faith. When Paul says, for example, that as Christians we have been "crucified with Christ" (Gal 2:20) and "baptized into his death" (Rom 6:3 NRSV), he is referring to what happens when we trust in Christ and Christ alone for salvation. No longer do we look to ourselves and our own works; no longer do we look to our keeping of God's commandments to make us right with God. Rather, we identify with him in his death. We trust in Christ's atoning death and that alone to save us. We come, in the words of the familiar hymn, "Just as I am, without one plea, but that thy blood was shed for me."[18]

This dimension of the cross in the life of the Christian is bound up with initial salvation, where we turn from sin and self and trust in Christ. In being crucified with Christ, we die to any and all of our own efforts to make ourselves righteous before God, and we look to Christ and Christ alone to save us.

So we must preach this dimension of the disciple's cross, for it establishes our salvation on a sure foundation: what Christ has done for us, not anything we have done.

Second, there is the cross of daily *self-denial*. Paul says that "those who belong to Christ Jesus have nailed the passions and desires of their sinful nature to his cross and crucified them there" (Gal 5:24). We don't hear much about it today, but what Paul is talking about here is the process of mortification, what Timothy George describes as "the daily putting to death of the flesh through the disciplines of prayer, fasting, repentance, and self-control."[19] In the pursuit of holiness, there is simply no substitute for this. Daily we must die to sin and be made alive to God. Paul also stresses that this daily putting to death is not primarily the result of human self-effort, but is the result of the Holy Spirit's working in us (Gal 5:16, 25; Rom 8:13).

What's more, says Paul, because of Christ's cross, "my interest in this world has been crucified, and the world's interest in me has also died" (Gal 6:14). Not only are we called to mortify the desires of our fallen sinful nature, but we must also renounce the values of the world system in which we live. Those aspects of our philosophy and worldview that still reflect the perspectives of this fallen world must be crucified as well.

Of course, in calling us to daily mortification and renunciation, Paul is only repeating what Jesus commanded his disciples: "If any of you wants to be my follower, you must turn from your selfish ways, take up your cross daily, and follow me" (Lk 9:23). This regular habit of taking up the cross through the daily practice of self-denial is not optional for Christians. Putting to death the deceitful desires of the flesh and renouncing the ways of the world is not only required of exceptional Christians—it is the basic requirement for every believer.

However, the cross we carry is not only limited to the self-

denial and discipline we place on ourselves. It is also composed of
the opposition and persecution imposed on us by others. This is
the third dimension of the Christian's cross: *suffering on behalf of
Christ.* Paul speaks about this cross often. He says that "our bodies
continue to share in the death of Jesus" (2 Cor 4:10) and that "I
bear on my body the scars that show I belong to Jesus" (Gal 6:17).
He also claims that he "face[s] death daily" (1 Cor 15:31) and that
"when I suffer for you in my body, . . . I am participating in the
sufferings of Christ that continue for his body, the church" (Col
1:24). He even considered it a privilege to be able to suffer for
Christ (Phil 1:29) and a cause for rejoicing (Phil 1:18). So he prays
that he might learn what it means "to suffer with him" (Phil
3:10).

Of course, the persecution we will experience can take various
forms—physical, intellectual, ethical or social. Thomas Smail
fleshes out some of the particular forms it can take:

> Christian believers who refuse to make a secret of their faith
> and try to follow its implications, positive and negative, in
> the lives they live among people every day will often find
> themselves estranged from their friends and even their fam-
> ilies as a result, denied advancement at work, subjected to
> subtle or not so subtle ridicule and ostracism in their social
> relationships, and faced with all kinds of clashes of loyalty
> where faithfulness to Christ will involve a refusal to follow
> the practices and expectations of those for whom they have
> regard or on whose favour they depend.[20]

There is a fourth dimension of the believer's cross; we might
call it the cross of *imitation*. Paul speaks about it in Philippians
3:10 when he expresses his desire to be conformed to Christ in his
death. To express this, Paul constructs a Greek verb by adding the
prefix *sym* (with) to the verb *morphizomenos*. It is the only time
the word is used in the New Testament, but it is Paul's way of ex-

pressing in the strongest way possible the close identification and intimate communion he has with Christ.

Derek Tidball suggests that Paul has in mind here the kind of growing together that one sees in couples who have been happily married for a long time. "They often think alike, react alike, enjoy the same things, share the same values, and copy each other's mannerisms." We too "come to think and act, judge and react, love and serve, trust and obey, pray and abide, submit and give, just as [Christ] did."[21] To be made conformable to his death is to be transformed into his likeness with ever-increasing glory (2 Cor 3:18). This, of course, is the work of his Spirit in us, but will only happen as we die to ourselves, praying with our Lord, "Not my will, but thy will be done" (see Mt 26:42).

The cross, then, is to be proclaimed not simply as a past event in the life of our Lord, but as a present reality in the life of every believer. Like Paul, all Christians are called to "suffer with him, sharing in his death" (Phil 3:10), to carry around in their bodies the death of Jesus so that the life of Jesus may also be seen in their bodies (2 Cor 4:10).

How crucial that in proclaiming these various dimensions of the disciple's cross, we preachers are a living embodiment of our message. For how can we invite others to take up their cross when, in our own lives, we are doing everything in our power to escape it? The disconnect, the contradiction between our manner of life and our message, will surely blunt the impact of our preaching. Calling others to a crucified life only makes sense when our hearers perceive that a living embodiment of that life is standing before them.

Not long ago such a preacher delivered a sermon in the seminary chapel where I teach. Her challenge to "come and die," aimed especially at our students preparing for ministry, could have been communicated more clearly and eloquently. At times she seemed to wander and get off message. She also made several extreme statements that caused the theologian in me to wince. *I know what she means,* I found myself thinking. *But if only she had said it in a more nuanced way. The way she expressed it can easily be misconstrued and misunderstood.*

And I was right. It was. The next day in my doctrine class, several students raised questions about her message and wanted clarification about certain things she had said. Her sermon, then, was by no means perfect. I could have given her several suggestions for improvement!

But the overall impact of her sermon and the response to her challenge to take up the cross was profound. I sat there at the end of chapel, deeply moved as I watched students stream to the altar to pray (though she had not actually given an altar call). It was evident to all that God was present in our midst. And I reflected on the fact that, more than anything she said, it was because of who she is that her message was so powerful and that God was able to use her in such profound ways. The marks of her own suffering and taking up the cross were so clear and unmistakable. Because she bears them in her own body, she is truly a living embodiment of her message.

May the same be said of us. May our calling others to take up the cross reflect and flow out of our first taking it up ourselves.

5

PREACHING THE RESURRECTION

NEW CREATION, LORDSHIP, VINDICATION

Easter was when Hope in person
surprised the whole world by coming forward
from the future into the present.

N. T. WRIGHT

It makes all the difference in the world whether someone is dead or alive. That's why, according to New Testament scholar Luke Timothy Johnson, the most important question about Jesus is whether he is dead or alive.[1] If he is dead, the memory of his life and accomplishments may still exert a significant influence, but his words and actions have ended. His life is over. Finished. Complete. The dead lie still.

But if he is alive, then everything is radically different. He can show up on our doorstep. Do new things. Surprise, confront, encourage, instruct us. Encounter us as one living person encounters another.

To be a Christian is to believe and confess that Jesus is alive. For everyone else, no matter how much he is admired, Jesus is still a dead man. For Christians he is the Living One. On this point, there can be no equivocating. It's either one or the other. As Johnson insists, "There is no middle ground between dead and alive. If Jesus is dead, then his story is completed. If he is alive, then his story continues."[2]

Every New Testament writer is firmly convinced that the story of Jesus continues. And they stake this cardinal conviction on the resurrection of Jesus. He is alive because God raised him from the dead. That's why the resurrection is front and center in the earliest apostolic preaching (Acts 2:29-36; 3:12-26; 5:29-32; 10:34-43; 13:16-41; 17:18, 22-31). Instead of following the logical order of the Christian year (Advent, Lent, Easter), they insist on preaching the gospel backward, beginning with Easter. Only then do they proceed to Christ's life, ministry and death, interpreting them in the light of his resurrection.

For the apostles, then, everything hinged upon Christ's resurrection. It was the first article of Christian faith and the foundation of all the rest. As Paul contends in 1 Corinthians 15, take away this cornerstone and the whole building collapses. Everything we've based our lives upon—our present faith in God, the forgiveness of sins past, our future hope—is an empty sham, nothing but smoke and mirrors, and we are "more to be pitied than anyone in the world" (1 Cor 15:19).

Most Christ followers and churchgoers today understand that the resurrection of Jesus matters. When they sing "Christ the Lord Is Risen Today," "Lord, I Lift Your Name on High" or "Christ Is Risen from the Dead" on Easter Sunday, like Americans in general, they mean it. According to a 1994 Harris poll, 87 percent of the American population believe in the resurrection.[3] But if you were to ask them why it matters and what it means, their answers would generally have little to do with the teaching of the New Testament.

In *The Lion, the Witch and the Wardrobe,* when Aslan comes back to life after being killed by the White Witch, Susan and Lucy aren't sure at first if he's really alive. Like the early disciples when the risen Christ stood in their midst on the first Easter (Lk 24:36-37), they wonder if Aslan is a ghost: "You're not—not a—?" asked Susan in a shaky voice. She couldn't bring herself to say the word *ghost.* Then Aslan licks her on the forehead, and when Susan feels the warmth of his breath and smells his hair, her doubts vanish. Immediately "both girls flung themselves upon him and covered him with kisses."[4] His unmistakable presence quickly dispels their doubts, and what a joyful reunion it is! Yet when they have calmed down, Susan, like a good theologian, wonders, "But what does it all mean?"[5]

CONTEMPORARY PREACHING OF THE RESURRECTION

Unfortunately, that's the question too much contemporary preaching of the resurrection fails to address. We know Christ's resurrection matters—if it didn't, we wouldn't celebrate Easter. But why does it matter? And what does it mean for us personally? for congregations? our world? all creation? We have generally failed to help our hearers grasp the profound, far-reaching meaning and significance the New Testament attaches to the resurrection.

Instead our Easter preaching has tended to move in other directions—two in particular. And even though on the surface they seem quite different, they share one thing in common. Both are the result of allowing the world around us, our current culture, to set the agenda for our preaching of the resurrection, rather than letting the New Testament itself determine it.

Overemphasizing apologetics. Confronted by scientists and philosophers outside the church who vehemently deny the resurrection, along with theologians within the church who reinterpret or demythologize it, we have spent so much time and effort defending the resurrection that we've hardly done anything else. To be sure, given the critics without and revisionists within the church, the apologetic task of making the case for the resurrection is something we have to do. Moreover, we owe a great debt to those biblical scholars, philosophers and theologians who have felt particularly called to do it.

Recently, no one has made the case more thoroughly and persuasively than New Testament scholar N. T. Wright. In his massive 817-page *The Resurrection of the Son of God*,[6] he carefully combs through the evidence confronting every major ancient and modern doubt about Easter. Wright also demonstrates how the early Christians' belief in the resurrection was rooted in two strongly held convictions: (1) Jesus' tomb was found empty on Easter morning, and (2) he then appeared to his followers alive and in bodily form. The best we can say about any ancient historical event is that there is a "high probability" it occurred. Based on those generally accepted criteria, Wright contends that the resurrection of Jesus qualifies as true. Given the best historical and circumstantial evidence, the empty tomb and the appearances are certainly plausible. Moreover, none of the other alternatives can explain the power and the spread of early Christianity.

Wright, no doubt, has made a convincing case for the resurrection. So have a number of others.[7] And surely, all of us should be profoundly grateful to them. But in the face of the resurrection's negative critics, ancient and modern, our preaching and teaching can get so caught up in defending the resurrection, making the case for the *what*, that we fail to adequately proclaim the *so what*, its positive meaning and significance for Christian faith today.

Overemphasizing life after death. In addition to overemphasizing apologetics in preaching the resurrection, there is also another approach we need to be careful not to fall into. Here, in keeping with the common cultural understanding, the resurrection is merely proclaimed as a timeless symbol for life and the triumph of life over death. Indeed, ask the average Christian to tell you what Jesus' resurrection means, and he or she will probably say, "Because Jesus died and rose, we know we will live after we die too." Easter thus becomes a spring festival associated with bunnies and eggs, with the leaves breaking forth after the dead of winter, butterflies emerging from chrysalises or tadpoles from dormant eggs. As a result, the resurrection is no longer seen as a unique and singular event on par with the event of original creation itself, but is viewed as another instance and piece of evidence for what has always been—that our souls are immortal so we live on after we die.

According to the New Testament, however, if there is one thing Christ's resurrection does *not* signify, it is that. As C. S. Lewis explains,

> There is not in Scripture the faintest suggestion that the Resurrection was new evidence for something that had *in fact* been always happening. The New Testament writers speak as if Christ's achievement in rising from the dead was the first event of its kind in the whole history of the universe. . . . He has forced open a door that has been locked since the death of the first man. He has met, fought, and beaten the King of Death. Everything is different because He has done so. This is the beginning of the New Creation: a new chapter in cosmic history has opened.[8]

Of course, we shouldn't be shocked or surprised that many Christians are unaware of this. Nature abhors a vacuum. So when preachers fail to communicate the meaning and significance the New Testament attaches to Easter, other meanings—some cultural, others common to religion in general—will soon get attached to it. If we don't articulate the meaning of the resurrection, rest assured our parishioners will do it themselves. In what follows, then, in this chapter and the next, we want to consider what the New Testament has to say about the significance of the resurrection. Each of these key ideas can and should provide us with important preaching themes.

RESURRECTION AND NEW CREATION

Let's start by underscoring the point C. S. Lewis makes in the statement above—that the resurrection of Jesus marks the beginning of new creation, "the first event of its kind in the whole history of the universe." In our discussion of preaching the cross, we stressed the need to help our congregations recover the original message of the cross as something scandalous, even revolting. Our task is to make something that has become so familiar—the wonderful, old rugged cross—become strange and unfamiliar.

We have a similar task in preaching the resurrection. Christians have tended to reduce the significance of the resurrection to the certainty of heaven and life after death. That's the meaning that is familiar. Especially at this particular point, then, in helping them understand the resurrection as the beginning of new creation, we have to make the familiar become unfamiliar again. In fact, we must help them understand how contrary their commonly held view is to the teaching of the New Testament.

When the apostles proclaimed that Jesus was raised from the dead, it certainly wasn't to announce there was a heavenly hereafter or a life beyond. After all, they were devout Jews, and like most devout Jews in their day, they already believed that. At death, they had been taught, the human soul was separated from the body and went to a shadowy world of the afterlife called *Sheol*.

When they did talk of "heaven" in terms of the particular place in *Sheol* where the souls of the righteous (as opposed to the unrighteous) lived on, it was never understood as their final destination or resting place but, according to N. T. Wright, "as a temporary stage on the way to the eventual resurrection of the body."[9] Consider, for example, when Jesus assures the thief on the cross that he will be with him in paradise (Lk 23:43), or when he declares to his disciples that there are many rooms in his Father's house (Jn 14:2), or when Paul expresses his desire to depart and be with the Lord (Phil 1:23). In each case, they are referring to that blissful place of life with the Lord beyond death. But they never associated or equated it with the resurrection of the dead. In their minds, this place was only a prelude to it.[10]

In keeping with the commonly held Jewish belief of their day, the early Christians adhered to "a two-step belief about the future."[11] First, life after death; then the resurrection of the body and the renewal of all creation (what Wright likes to call "life after life after death"). Furthermore, they certainly never mixed up these two steps or equated them with each other.

Thus *before* Jesus' resurrection, they already adhered to a firm belief in the resurrection of the dead. However, it had little to do with the realm of the dead and the transitional place where the souls of the righteous go after they die. Rather, they associated resurrection of the dead with the Day of the Lord, the Last Day, the age to come and the final restoration of all things. When Jesus, for example, assures Martha that her brother, Lazarus, will rise again, her initial response reflects the typical Jewish view: "Yes, . . . he will rise when everyone else rises, at the last day" (Jn 11:24).

What was so stunning, then, to the early Christians about the resurrection of Jesus was *not* that God could raise the dead. Like Martha, they *already* believed in a general resurrection when God would raise the righteous at the last day. What stunned them and sent them reeling was the timing of it. In the case of Jesus, the general resurrection, which was supposed to happen on the last day, had moved forward from the end into the present. What was supposed to happen on the final day had happened now. According to Neville Clark, "He is risen!" meant that "the Last Day at the end of history had taken shape on the third day in the midst of history."[12] In other words, tomorrow had happened today!

God's new world, the new heavens and new earth, had come into being through the resurrection of Jesus of Nazareth. The promise of a renewed covenant, which Jeremiah (Jer 31) and Ezekiel (Ezek 36) described, where sins would be forgiven and death would be no more, had actually begun. The transformation of the whole cosmos, the new creation, foretold by the prophet Isaiah (Is 60–66) to happen at the end of time, had already started. The resurrection of Jesus was therefore not only one miracle—extraordinary no doubt—among others; nor was it simply the final guarantee of life after death. Rather, it was the decisive start of the general resurrection, God's final redemption of all things!

To be sure, Christ's resurrection was not to be confused with the *completion* of final redemption. Jesus had been raised from the dead, and that marked "the beginning of the end." But his followers certainly hadn't likewise been raised. That would happen later at "the end of the end," when Jesus would return in glory. As Paul explains in 1 Corinthians 15:23: "But there is an order to this resurrection: Christ was raised as the first of the harvest; then all who belong to Christ will be raised when he comes back."

As a result, in Wright's words, "The Jewish expectation of resurrection—the resurrection of all God's people at the end of time—has been split into two: first an advance foretaste, then the rest to follow. The Messiah has been raised as the start of the general resurrection; those who belong to him will be raised at his final appearing. Then and only then will he complete the implementation of the victory he won at Calvary and Easter."[13]

In the meantime, those who belong to Christ live between the beginning and the end of the end times, between the *already* future and the *not yet* future. Because Jesus has been raised, the future, the life of the age to come, has *already* dawned. Through the certainty of sins forgiven, the presence of the Holy Spirit, the joy of life in Christ and fellowship in his body, we have been given a foretaste of that future now.

But we also live in hope and anticipation of the *not yet* future. Jesus has not yet returned or descended from heaven with a shout (1 Thess 4:16). Suffering, evil, death and decay are still all around. As Paul expresses it, "While we live in these earthly bodies, we groan and sigh" (2 Cor 5:4). The enemies of Christ rage against us and refuse to acknowledge he is Lord; they have not yet been made into a footstool for his feet. So we long for the completion of final resurrection, the redemption of our bodies, the fullness of new creation, the subjugation of all Christ's enemies, the restoration of all things. And our hearts cry, "Amen! Come, Lord Jesus" (Rev 22:20).

By now, however, you may be wondering, "Why is it important to hammer this point home in our preaching? Resurrection as new creation—it's an important and inspiring theological point and certainly taught in the New Testament, but what practical difference does it make in our personal lives and in our congregations, anyway?" So let me spell it out as clearly and as forthrightly as I can.

Often our preaching of the resurrection has focused almost exclusively on our personal, individual selves and the question of what happens to us after we die. That, of course, is a pertinent question as well as a biblical one (Job 14:14). But in terms of what the New Testament has to say about the resurrection of Jesus, it's not the primary, overarching question at all. As Wright maintains, "The New Testament, true to its Old Testament roots, regularly insists that the major, central, framing question is that of God's purpose or rescue and re-creation for the whole world, the entire cosmos."[14]

The point is, God's plan of redemption in Christ is not primarily about you and me and our personal redemption. It's about the redemption of *all* creation. Our individual future, as significant as that is, must be understood in the context of the whole creation's future, not the other way around. Understanding this, in turn, has profound implications for our present lives. Our purpose is not only to live righteously so we can attain our personal heavenly reward in the afterlife. Our purpose is to be engaged in preparing ourselves, yes, *but also* our community and our world—indeed, the *whole* world—for its destined future.

The resurrection of Jesus has therefore set in motion the final redemption and transformation of all creation. As believers we are called to participate in that process, to lean toward the future as we long with all of creation for its ultimate redemption (Rom 8:18-25). And as we anticipate that redemption, to work concretely toward personal, community, social and cosmic transformation in keeping with creation's true and final destiny.

Of course, this doesn't mean we ourselves can usher in the new creation. That will only happen when our Lord returns. But we are called to work toward that end in the present. Our salvation and mission and destiny must therefore be seen in the light of this goal. Again, N. T. Wright captures the heart of the New Testament understanding and its implications for us:

> Because the early Christians believed that resurrection had begun with Jesus and would be completed in the great final resurrection on the last day, they believed that God had called them to work with him, in the power of the Spirit, to implement the achievement of Jesus and thereby to anticipate the final resurrection, in personal and political life, in mission and holiness. It was not merely that God had inaugurated the "end"; if Jesus, the Messiah, was the End in person, God's-future-arrived-in-the-present, then those who belonged to Jesus and followed him and were empowered by His Spirit were charged with transforming the present, as far as they were able, in the light of the future.[15]

Transforming the present in the light of the future—that's what we're called to do, and our Easter preaching should challenge our congregations to think about it. What concretely might that mean for our church? Where specifically are we being summoned to do that?

At the beginning of this book we diagnosed the problem of the American Jesus who, both in the broader culture and the typical church, is presented primarily in terms of what he can do for us. We cited David Bryant's description of the problem—that the American church is willing to make Christ central (his right to be at the center of our personal and congregational worlds) but *not* supreme (his right to take us to the center of his world).[16]

Unfortunately, our preaching of the resurrection, by focusing more on *our* personal world and future than on *Christ's* new creation world and its future, has both reflected and reinforced the American Jesus problem. By repeatedly making the connection between resurrection and new creation, we are therefore striking a blow at the root of this problem. We are declaring that Christ is not only central, but supreme. In effect, we are proclaiming he is Lord of all. And that segues nicely to our next major preaching theme related to the resurrection.

JESUS IS LORD AND GOD

The early Christians boldly proclaimed that "Jesus is Lord." *Kurios Christos*—through these simple, straightforward words, a group of devout, fiercely monotheistic Jews dared to transfer to Jesus of Nazareth the divine name and title "Lord" (Hebrew, *Adonai*; Greek, *Kurios*), previously reserved exclusively for Yahweh, the God of Israel. This was the earliest, most primitive Christian confession, and what distinguished a believer from an unbeliever. A Christian was one who had called on the name of the Lord (Rom 10:13; 1 Cor 1:2; 6:11) and confessed "Jesus is Lord" (Rom 10:9).

Christ's lordship and the resurrection. From the very beginning, they staked their belief in Christ's lordship on his resurrection from the dead. That God had raised him was the surest proof he had been exalted and installed as Lord. As Peter declares in his Pentecost-day sermon, "God raised Jesus from the dead, and we are all witnesses of this. Now he is exalted to the place of highest honor in heaven, at God's right hand. . . . So let everyone in Israel know for certain that God has made this Jesus, whom you crucified, to be both Lord and Messiah!" (Acts 2:32-33, 36; see also 5:30-31).

Paul makes the same point throughout his letters. In Ephesians, for example, he extols God's mighty power that "raised Christ from the dead and seated him in the place of honor at God's right hand in the heavenly realms" (Eph 1:20). Similarly in Philippians, citing what many believe was an early Christian hymn, he declares that "God elevated him to the place of highest honor and gave him the name above all other names, that at the name of Jesus every knee should bow, in heaven and on earth and under the earth, and every tongue confess that Jesus Christ is Lord, to the glory of God the Father" (Phil 2:9-11).

Notice too, in his letter to the Romans, how he repeatedly makes the connection between Christ's lordship and his resurrection:

> He was shown to be the Son of God when he was raised from the dead by the power of the Holy Spirit. He is Jesus Christ our Lord. (Rom 1:4)

> If you confess with your mouth that Jesus is Lord and believe in your heart that God raised him from the dead, you will be saved. (Rom 10:9)

In many different languages, Christians throughout the world today sing a simple little chorus: "He is Lord, He is Lord! He has risen from the dead, and he is Lord. Every knee shall bow, every tongue confess, that Jesus Christ is Lord." Whenever they do, whether they realize it or not, they are making the connection too.

In our preaching we need to remind congregations of that. The exalted Lord is the Risen One. And he is exalted because he is risen. Take away his resurrection and you take away his lordship.

What's more, because *Lord* has become such a familiar, commonly used title for Jesus, we need to spell out its significance so that our hearers grasp the full force of it. In *The Theology of the Resurrection* (1933), Walter Kunneth, a theologian who was a leader of the Confessing Church in Germany that stood against Hitler, suggests that in the New Testament the title has a twofold meaning.

First, *Lord* (*Kurios*) indicates "the unconditional claim of God in the face of the whole universe."[17] Such a claim, Kunneth explains, includes *cosmic* lordship. As the one through whom all things were made (Jn 1:3; Col 1:16) and are held together (Col 1:17), he has absolute power over all created things. Furthermore, it includes *moral* lordship over the conscience of every human being. He has the right to place moral demands on us. It also includes *community* lordship. He is the King of Israel (Jn 1:49) and the head of the church (Col 1:18) and exercises divine lordship over the community of believers.[18] Lordship, therefore, extends over every sphere of creation, every knee and tongue, every height and depth. No cosmic, societal, communal or personal space stands outside of it. He is Lord of all, period. Consequently, as Abraham Kuyper declares, "There is not one square inch of the entire creation about which Jesus Christ does not cry out, 'This is mine! This belongs to me!' "[19]

Second, lordship signifies, in addition to God's unconditional claim, God's *absolute* claim on us. He is Lord in all things and in every situation. That means there can be no other lords. He will tolerate no rivals. Thus all other forms of lordship are either *derived* (ordained and empowered by him) or *presumptuous* (the result of rebellion). As Kunneth puts it, "He who is Kyrios is absolute Lord. His lordship is valid for every sphere and all ages;

nothing can evade its claim."[20]

Jesus is God. Given the twofold significance of the title *Lord,* when transferred and conferred upon the Risen Jesus, it means that he now stands in the very place of God. What God does in exercising unconditional and absolute lordship, now Jesus does. The lordship he exercises is therefore a *divine* lordship, and he exercises such lordship because he is, in fact, divine. In Karl Barth's words, "'Jesus is the Lord' means 'Jesus is God.' 'The Lord is Jesus' means 'God is Jesus.'"[21]

He is fully divine—declared to be Son of God by his resurrection from the dead (Rom 1:4)—therefore his lordship is fully divine. It is therefore *extensive*—over all creation, all persons, all things, all times and places. But it is also *intensive*—as full and as perfect and as ultimate as God's lordship itself. Christ's lordship is God's lordship, and God's lordship is Christ's. One is never different from or higher than the other.

In discussing whether Christians should eat food offered to idols, Paul reminds the Corinthians of this. Others worship many gods, he says, and acknowledge many lords. "But we know that there is only one God, the Father, who created everything, and we live for him. And there is only one Lord, Jesus Christ, through whom God made everything and through whom we have been given life" (1 Cor 8:6).

Lordship and divinity, like two columns of a magnificent arch, are therefore inseparable and dependent on each other. And the keystone of the arch is the resurrection of Christ. Take that away and both columns—in fact, the entire structure—tumbles down. Notice how Paul brings all three together at the beginning of his letter to the Romans. The gospel he has been commissioned to preach, he says, is about God's Son, Jesus, who was "shown to be the Son of God when he was raised from the dead by the power of the Holy Spirit. He is Jesus Christ our Lord" (Rom 1:4).

When the Christian movement first began, Paul *never* would

have said that. In fact, he was hell-bent on persecuting any Jewish follower of Jesus, like Stephen, who dared to make such a blasphemous claim. But then, on the road to Damascus, he had a dramatic personal encounter with the risen Jesus himself. As Jesus had appeared to the other apostles earlier, now Paul "also saw him" (1 Cor 15:8), and that changed everything. "Who are you, lord?" he asked (Acts 9:5). "I am Jesus, the one you are persecuting," the risen Christ answered. A few days later Paul began preaching about Jesus in the synagogues in Damascus, declaring, "He is indeed the Son of God!" (Acts 9:20). So we see how lordship, resurrection and Son of God were all bound up in Paul's own Christian experience from the very beginning.

They also all come together in Jesus' resurrection appearance to Thomas. Earlier when he had first appeared to the disciples, Thomas was absent, so he was unconvinced that Jesus was alive. "I won't believe it," he adamantly declared, "unless I see the nail wounds in his hands, put my fingers into them, and place my hand into the wound in his side" (Jn 20:25).

Eight days later, however, when Jesus appeared to the disciples again, Thomas was present. Jesus turned to Thomas and invited him to do exactly what he had demanded: "Put your finger here, and look at my hands. Put your hand into the wound in my side" (Jn 20:27). In that moment it all clicked! Thomas realized Jesus must have heard him earlier when he had expressed his doubts to the others. How else did he know so exactly what Thomas had demanded? He was alive then. He is alive now! That must mean it *is* true—he is risen from the dead. And that must mean, as Thomas exclaimed, "My Lord and my God!" (Jn 20:28).

How fitting it is, then, on Easter and the Sundays that follow, to proclaim the lordship and divinity of Christ. According to Andrew Purves, "In the light of the resurrection of Jesus the central task of Christian preaching is to proclaim that Jesus is Lord because Jesus lives."[22] What better time, then, to raise the all-important question, Who do you say that I am? (Mk 8:27-30). And to let the empty tomb, the reality of the resurrection, provide the indisputable answer: He is Lord and God.

Implications of Christ's lordship. But let's not stop there. Let's go on to draw out the far-reaching personal, communal, societal and cosmic implications of Christ's lordship. Because he is Lord and God, he has the right to make claims on our personal lives. So he summons us to follow him, even when it means taking up the cross. Each one of us, willingly or unwillingly, has to answer to him. In fact, ultimately the question will *not* be, Who do you say Jesus is? but, What will Jesus say about you? When he returns, he will stand in judgment over us. As Paul told the Athenians, God has set a day for rightly judging the world by a man he has appointed, and "he proved to everyone who this is by raising him from the dead" (Acts 17:31).

Because Jesus is Lord and God, he is also Lord of the church. Every local congregation belongs to him. We don't tell him what to do—he tells us! He is the One we worship, the One who sets our agenda, the One who stands in judgment over us. As he addressed the seven churches (Rev 2–3)—praising, encouraging, revealing, admonishing, warning, judging, calling, promising—so he addresses us. He is Lord of the church. As a congregation, are we listening to him? Obeying him? Following him? Loving him?

Jesus is also Lord over governments and states, over nations, societies, and cultures—including ours. Unfortunately, in American "God and country" civil religion, Jesus often gets wrapped up in an American flag. Preaching this crucial dimension of Christ's lordship will therefore take courage and boldness combined with deep wisdom. Declaring that our nation—its morality, economy, military, legal system, domestic and foreign policies—must answer and bow to him will make many in our congregations uncomfortable. Some will find it threatening. Our preaching may sound strange, un-American and unpatriotic. "Why are you being so political? Why are you mixing religion with politics?" some will ask. "Just stick to preaching the gospel."

The truth is, proclaiming the lordship of Christ over nations and states has always caused sparks to fly. During the apostolic age, you merely had to confess "Jesus is Lord" to do it. Imperial Rome proclaimed that "Caesar is Lord." To confess that "Jesus is Lord" meant Caesar wasn't. The state considered it an act of sedition and high treason punishable by death. To proclaim "He is risen" meant "He is Lord." That meant Rome had to answer to him, bow down to him and be judged by him—not the other way around.

Governments, and especially tyrants—from Herod to Hitler—instinctively know this. They are always threatened by the resurrection because it means their greatest weapon, fear of death and destruction, is no longer omnipotent. In Oscar Wilde's wonderful play *Salome,* wily Herod hears reports that Jesus has been raising people from the dead. "I do not wish him to do that," he says. "I forbid him to do that. I allow no man to raise the dead. This man must be found and told that I forbid him to raise the dead."[23]

According to Karl Barth,[24] this is what is really behind *all* denials of the resurrection. Ultimately, they are denials of Christ's lordship and attempts to evade his lordship over us. We stubbornly refuse to answer to anyone but ourselves. By denying his resurrection and therefore his lordship, we deny his right to reign over us.

RIGHTEOUSNESS VINDICATED

Jesus was *exalted* as Lord and *designated* to be the Son of God through his resurrection from the dead (Rom 1:4). Easter is therefore God's resounding Yes to the ministry of Jesus. Three days earlier everyone in Jerusalem had said No to Jesus. The religious authorities tried and convicted him, Pilate condemned and sentenced him, the common people scorned and rejected him, and his own disciples betrayed and deserted him. God seemed to have abandoned him too. The fact that he had been nailed to a cross, experienced horrific pain and suffering, and died as a sinner under God's curse confirmed their verdict on Jesus. It proved this Galilean peasant was no Messiah, but just another pretender in a long line of pretenders.

Easter Sunday, however, proved how dead wrong these assumptions were. The resurrection settled the matter once and for all. God reversed the grave injustice inflicted upon Jesus and pronounced that the rejected, crucified Jesus was in fact the righteous one. Proclaiming the resurrection as a vindication of the righteousness of Jesus was therefore a prominent theme in early Christian preaching and apologetics (Acts 2:23-24; 3:15; 4:10; 5:30). "You nailed him to a cross and killed him," Peter declared to the people of Jerusalem in his Pentecost sermon (Acts 2:23). "But God raised him from the dead." Later he accused the Jewish leaders of doing the same thing (Acts 4:10). "The stone that you builders rejected," Peter insisted, "has now become the cornerstone" (Acts 4:11).

The resurrection, then, is a vindication of the righteousness of Christ. It is God's great reversal; the Father's amen to the life, ministry and death of his Son. As Jürgen Moltmann explains, "If God raised Jesus, he puts all those who condemned, abandoned and crucified him in the wrong. Then the raising of the One crucified is the divine justification of Jesus of Nazareth and his message, for which he was put to death."[25]

Bound up with this are two other corollary New Testament teachings. First, the vindication of Christ through his resurrection is the basis for and pointer to the ultimate vindication when Christ returns to judge and to rule (Acts 17:31). The future, when "he shall come to judge the living and the dead," will fully and finally unfold what Easter already means in the present. Christ is risen and is seated *now* at God's right hand. He has been given all power and authority and has begun to judge and rule (Eph 1:19-23). Thus when he returns to judge, as J. F. Jansen expresses it, "This 'last' judgment is but the unfolding of the 'past' judgment."[26]

Second, because Jesus was vindicated by his resurrection, those who faithfully follow him can be sure they will be vindicated too. Though now they may be enduring fiery trials or suffering for righteousness, the resurrection is the ground of their hope. Jesus was the righteous sufferer who was abandoned by everyone. He even felt abandoned by God. Yet he trusted God and cried out for vindication, believing that God would not leave his holy and righteous one in distress (Acts 3:14). And on the *third* day—considered by the Jews to be the day of deliverance and vindication (Hos 6:2)—God raised him up. God vindicated Jesus and will likewise vindicate those who faithfully persevere in following him.

In our congregations there are always those suffering for the sake of righteousness who are tempted to give up. *What's the use in being faithful to God and doing what is right?* they sometimes find themselves thinking. *Take the path of least resistance. Look out for yourself. Do whatever's necessary to get ahead. That's what everyone else is doing.* Preach, then, on this theme to provide them assurance and hope, and to encourage them to persevere and stand firm. As Paul concludes his great resurrection sermon in 1 Corinthians 15, "So, my dear brothers and sisters, be strong and immovable. Always work enthusiastically for the Lord, for you know that nothing you do for the Lord is ever useless" (1 Cor 15:58).

We should preach the resurrection not only as a vindication of *Christ's* righteousness and the righteousness of his followers, but also as the vindication of *God's* righteousness. For how could God have allowed the violent, ignominious death of such a righteous, innocent one? How could God stand there and do nothing in the face of such a gross miscarriage of justice? If, in fact, God had done nothing, it would surely have called his righteousness into question.

A six-year-old boy was getting increasingly upset as he heard

Mrs. Hansen, his Sunday school teacher, vividly describe the passion of Christ. First, how he was mistreated at his trial by the Jewish leaders. Then, how Pilate had him flogged with a lead-tipped whip. And finally, how his hands and feet were nailed to a cruel cross. His eyes kept getting bigger and bigger, and he was becoming more agitated. It was so wrong and unfair. He couldn't believe they had done such terrible things to such a kind and innocent man. How could they get away with it? Finally, he couldn't stand it any longer and blurted out, "Mrs. Hansen, Mrs. Hansen, where the hell was the state police when all this was going on?"

Forget about the state police—where was *God* when the holy, righteous and innocent one, his very own Son, was being crucified? Even in death Jesus trusted God to deliver him and raise him up. Yet if God simply stood by and did nothing, when the most righteous man who had ever lived was mistreated like this, what does that say about God's righteousness? And what about God's love? How can we trust in it? Doesn't God *care* about his son? Or God's power? Can't God *do* something to help him?

As A. M. Hunter expresses it, "If the story of Jesus ends there (at the Cross), then it is an unmitigated tragedy and—what is more—the supreme proof of the irrationality of the universe in which we live."[27] Without the resurrection, as Paul insists, our faith is useless (1 Cor 15:14). Trusting in God and doing his will in the face of opposition—when everyone is standing against you, when God himself seems to have abandoned you—turns out to be a cruel, sick joke.

"But in fact, Christ has been raised from the dead" (1 Cor 15:20). And that means—though everything in my world and our world seems like Good Friday—we must hold on, hang on and hope on, because Easter Sunday's coming! There is a God in heaven, and regardless of how evil seems to triumph, his kingdom *will* come on earth as it is in heaven. As the hymn writer says, "This is my Father's world, O let me n'er forget that though the wrong seems oft so strong, God is the ruler yet."[28]

Good Friday certainly raised questions about God's character—his righteousness, love, sovereignty and power. But Easter Sunday raised the man Christ Jesus. And the raised man is the answer to all the raised questions.

That's what the two men on the road to Emmaus came to realize. They were confused and heartbroken. The one who they thought was the Messiah who had come to rescue Israel had been handed over by their religious leaders and condemned to an ignominious death. How could a good God allow such a thing to happen? But the stranger who had joined them as they walked challenged them to think differently: "Wasn't it clearly predicted that the Messiah would have to suffer all these things before entering his glory?" (Lk 24:26). God's ways, they came to see, were profoundly different from theirs.

But it was when their eyes were opened and they recognized the stranger as the risen Christ that everything really changed. "Didn't our hearts burn within us as he talked with us on the road and explained the Scriptures to us?" (Lk 24:32). Within an hour they were back in Jerusalem telling the disciples the good news: "The Lord has really risen!" (Lk 24:34).

Philosopher Stephen Davis maintains that is "the best piece of news the world has ever heard." Why? Because:

> It assures us that God will win in the end and that accordingly the world is not mad. Events do happen that we cannot explain. Irrational tragedies and horrible outrages do occur. But because God raised Jesus from the dead after the catastrophe of the cross, we can be sure that God will one day overcome all catastrophes. . . . The resurrection is proof that no matter how bad things get, we can trust in God. God loves us. God has our interests at heart. God works to achieve what is beneficial to us. And in the end God will win.[29]

6

PREACHING
THE RESURRECTION

CHURCH, SALVATION, LIFE EVERLASTING

The Church of Christ is not an institution;
she is a new life with Christ and in Christ,
directed by the Holy Spirit.
The light of the Resurrection of Christ
shines on the Church, which is filled with the joy
of the Resurrection, of triumph over death.
The risen Lord lives with us
and our life in the Church is a life of mystery in Christ.

SERGEI BULGAKOV

It makes all the difference in the world, we said, whether Jesus is dead or alive. Everything stands or falls on that. So far we've seen how what Christians believe about final redemption (new creation), the person of Christ (Jesus is Lord!) and the character of God (righteous, loving and powerful) are all grounded in the reality of the resurrection. Our preaching must spell out the connection between the resurrection and each of these core beliefs in a clear and compelling way. But we're not finished! There's more to be taught and preached about the resurrection. So in this chapter, let's see how what we believe about church, salvation and life everlasting are all rooted in the resurrection too.

THE COMMUNITY OF THE RESURRECTION

Say the word *church*, and people think "building," "religious organization," "community," "fellowship," "voluntary association," "denomination" or "institution." But according to the New Testament, we should first think "body of Christ." As Paul reminds the Corinthians, "All of you together are Christ's body, and each of you is a part of it" (1 Cor 12:27; see also Rom 12:5; 1 Cor 10:16; Eph 2:22-23; 4:12; 5:23; Col 1:18, 24). Although the New Testament uses other significant images to describe the church, none is as foundational and pivotal as this one. As Thomas Oden maintains, "the body of Christ remains a more concise definition of the church than any other descriptive phrase."[1]

Most Christians are at least vaguely familiar with the phrase. If you asked for an explicitly biblical or theological description of the church, someone would say, "The church is the body of Christ." But what exactly does it mean? Ask that, and most likely you get an answer that has little to do with the New Testament understanding. Although most Christians are familiar with the phrase, they can't fill it with any specific biblical meaning.

So what did the apostle Paul, the New Testament writer who repeatedly uses this phrase, mean by it? And what caused him to use it in the first place? Once again, we find ourselves led back to the resurrection, and particularly Paul's own dramatic encounter when the risen Christ appeared to him on the Damascus road.

According to the narrative in Acts, Saul (he was not Paul yet) was "going everywhere to destroy the church" (Acts 8:1-3). That's why he was on his way to Damascus—to stamp out the church there. Approaching the city, he was blinded by a light from heaven and fell to the ground. An unfamiliar voice addressed him: "Saul! Saul! Why are you persecuting me?" (Acts 9:4; 22:7; 26:14). When he asked "Who are you, lord?" the answer was unequivocal: "I am Jesus, the one you are persecuting" (Acts 9:5).

Some scholars maintain that Paul's use of the phrase "body of Christ" stems from his Damascus road encounter with the risen Lord, particularly what he heard when he asked the voice to identify itself. Until this point in the narrative, Saul has been leading the persecution against the fledgling *church,* but now the risen Christ insists that *he* is the one Saul is persecuting. "Why are you persecuting *me*?" "I am Jesus, *the one you are persecuting*" (Acts 9:4-5, italics mine). When you persecute the church, Saul is told, you are directly—not indirectly—persecuting Christ himself. That's how close the connection is between the risen Lord and his followers. Later when Paul pens his epistles and identifies the church as the body of Christ, he intends to say the same thing.

We sometimes use the word *body* in the sense of a corporate body, to refer to a group or a collection of people. For example, "Let's vote and determine what the will of the body is on this matter." But that's *not* what Paul has in mind in calling the church the body of Christ. As David van Daalen explains, "Paul uses the word differently, not in a corporate but in a corporal sense: he is referring, not to a society but to a person, namely Christ." The notion that people could be members of a corporate body or group, he notes, would not have been strange or difficult for Paul's readers to fathom. "But the idea of people, i.e. the believers, being parts of another person's body must have seemed absurd. Yet this is precisely how Paul uses the expression."[2]

So when Paul says, "You are the body of Christ," he *doesn't* mean, "You are a part of a *corporate* body of people who are together seeking to follow Christ." What he does mean is, "You are a part of Christ's very own *corporal* body." And, of course, that only makes sense if Christ has been raised from the dead. That is, if he is alive—not as a ghost or some sort of spiritual, ethereal force—and if he has a resurrection *body* as well.

When we come to faith in Christ through the Holy Spirit, we actually become a part of his resurrected body. As Paul says, "we have all been baptized into one body by one Spirit" (1 Cor 12:13). Moreover, as Karl Barth insists, what makes the body of Christ a body is not primarily the various parts or the way they are connected to each other. What makes it a body is the One who holds it together and governs it.[3] That Jesus is the head of the church and that we as believers are parts of his body means, first and foremost, that he is the one who binds us together and governs us, both as parts and as the whole.[4]

Moreover, it is his very own life, his resurrected life, in which we share and participate. This is what makes the church essentially a living organism, not an organization. In an organism—plant, animal or human—all the cells share a common life. Likewise in the body of Christ, all the parts, regardless how distinct and diverse they are, share a common life: the life of our risen Lord.

"The church," Dietrich Bonhoeffer often stressed, "is Christ existing as community."[5] As incarnate Lord, he became an individual flesh-and-blood person and assumed a body. But as our risen Lord, he is both an *individual* person with a glorified body and, according to Bonhoeffer, a *corporate* person with a body, the church, through which he lives and governs and ministers. So we should think of the church "not as an institution, but as a *person,* though, of course, a person in a unique sense."[6]

Apart from the resurrection none of this makes any sense. Because if there is no resurrection, there is no risen life of Christ to share in and no living head of the church who governs and leads. All that's left is a religious *organization*—at best a *corporate* body centered around Christ, held together by common memories, traditions, values and goals. But not an *organism* where all members share a common life, or a *corporal* body where each member is a part of Christ's body.

That's why we must preach about this crucial connection between resurrection and church. When we fail to understand it, the church is reduced to a human religious institution and inevitably becomes more about us than it is about Christ. We, the members and parts of the body, end up taking control of its leadership and setting its goals. Human initiative and energy fuel its life. It becomes "our church," "the pastor's church," "that family's church" or "my church" more than Christ's. The hymn writer is right: "The Church's *one* foundation is Jesus Christ her Lord"[7] (italics mine). How often we need to be reminded of that!

THE MISSION OF THE CHURCH

The resurrection not only determines the nature of the church; it also shapes its threefold mission: worshiping God, building up believers and redeeming the world. Consider how the resurrection of Christ is crucial in understanding the nature of each.

Worshiping God. "For where two or three gather together because they are mine, I am there among them" (Mt 18:20). When we come together, the Lord Jesus promises to be personally present in our midst. So when we gather for worship, we invoke his presence, give him praise and thanks, confess our sins to him, address him in prayer, listen as he speaks, receive his empowering, and depart with his blessing. From start to finish, our worship is Christ-centered. That's why although most of the earliest Christians were devout Jews, they soon changed their day of worship from the Sabbath to the first day of the week and called it the Lord's Day (Acts 20:7; 1 Cor 16:2; Rev 1:10). Worship on Sunday, the first day of the week, the day of resurrection, was an anticipated time of meeting together with the risen Lord Jesus and with each other. Every Sunday was looked on as an Easter Sunday.

In the sermon or homily, while a human preacher proclaims

God's word, the risen Christ is also with us. His promised presence with us is the reason we preach in the first place. As Thomas Long maintains, "Preaching in the name of Christ is possible only because Christ is already present, because Christ has already decided to be with us, because Christ has already chosen to meet us in the spoken word of our preaching."[8] He himself speaks to us through the broken, stumbling preacher's words. He is the head of the church, and just as he had a message for each of the seven churches in the first century (Rev 2–3), so he has a word for us and our local churches today. Ultimately, then, our task as preachers is to allow ourselves to be taken command of by the risen Christ so that he can speak to our community through us.

In the Lord's Supper, the risen Christ also meets with his people. He was known to the two men on the road to Emmaus "as he was breaking the bread" (Lk 24:35). So too is he known to us. In the Lord's Supper we not only remember his passion, but we also celebrate his living presence. It is both a "last supper" and an Easter meal. When the final benediction is pronounced by the pastor, Jesus our great High Priest, like the Old Testament priests (Num 6:22-27), is blessing his people. From start to finish, then, our worship assumes that Jesus is alive and well and active in our midst.

Building up believers. The resurrection also defines the nature of Christian fellowship. For our *koinonia,* as the New Testament calls it (Acts 2:42; Phil 1:5; 1 Jn 1:3-6), is not merely human camaraderie, compassion or cohesiveness. Because we share the common life of our risen Lord, our connection to each other is much deeper. We have *koinonia* (fellowship) with him and therefore *koinonia* with each other. John the apostle says that we proclaim him, the "Word of life, . . . so that you may have fellowship with us. And our fellowship is with the Father and with his Son, Jesus Christ" (1 Jn 1:1, 3).

C. S. Lewis's good friend Charles Williams coined the phrase

"company of the coinherence"[9] to describe the church. We belong
to each other because we belong to him. And by the way, this includes our fellowship, our communion with saints on earth (the
church on earth) and our "mystic sweet communion"[10] with the
departed saints who have gone before us (the church in heaven).
He lives in us; we live in him. And the relationship we have with
each other flows out of the relationship we have in common with
the living Christ.

Redeeming the world. The church's mission and ministry are
also rooted in the resurrection. Because Christ is alive, his ministry continues and so does his mission. That means, as Andrew
Purves insists, "Jesus is not our cheerleader from the heavens hop-
ing we will get faith and ministry right. . . . Rather, Jesus has his
own ministry to do . . . *and he wants us in on it.*"[11] He is still present
and working and is the principal actor in mission. Thus when the
risen Christ commissions his disciples to "go and make disciples
of all the nations," he assures them, "I am with you always, even
to the end of the age" (Mt 28:19-20).

He is with us and goes before us. All of the church's mission
and ministry is essentially a participation in the ongoing ministry
of our risen Lord. Again, Andrew Purves articulates it well: "To
participate in Christ's ministry means we share in his *life.* Who he
is and what he is up to defines the whole work of our ministry.
Wherever Christ is, there is the ministry of the church. . . . *It is not
our ministries that make Christ present and possible: it is the present,
living Christ who makes our ministries possible.*"[12]

In 1865, while Hudson Taylor was on furlough in England after
serving as a missionary in China for six years, the risen Christ
spoke to him: "I am going to evangelize inland China, and if you
will walk with me, I will do it through you."[13] He went on to found
the China Inland Mission, and thirty years later it numbered 691
missionaries serving in all of China's provinces except for several
border regions. Through them (and there were many others too!)

the risen Christ began a work in evangelizing the interior of China that continues today.

David Aikman tells the amazing story of what's been going on in China in his book with an apt title: *Jesus in Beijing*.[14] For that's the nature of the church's mission in Beijing, as well as everywhere else. Not working *for* Christ, but working *with* him in his ongoing mission as he accomplishes his resurrected ministry through us.

Preach the resurrection, then, as foundational to the mission of the church. If we fail to understand that, the church is reduced to a human enterprise. Then everything is cast back on us—what we can do for him, instead of what he can do through us—and when that happens, we're in trouble—big trouble.

SALVATION MEANS SHARING IN CHRIST'S RISEN LIFE

Earlier we said that for many Christians, the meaning of Easter has *only* to do with life after death. Since Christ was raised on the third day, there'll come a day when we'll be raised too. Christ's resurrection therefore guarantees our future hope. Yet as true to biblical teaching as that is, the New Testament writers also insist that resurrection has *everything* to do with our lives in the present as well.

For the believer, experiencing the power of Christ's resurrection begins here and now. The moment we put our faith in Christ and are joined to him, we share in his resurrection. In fact, from start to finish, from initial to final salvation, the believer's new life in Christ involves participation in his risen life.

At the point of baptism—the outward sign of our being joined to Christ and initiated into the Christian life—Paul tells the Roman believers, "we died and were buried with Christ. . . . And just as Christ was raised from the dead by the glorious power of the Father, now we also may live new lives" (Rom 6:4; cf. Col 2:12). Our new lives in Christ are the result of a new birth, a regeneration, a death and resurrection that has taken place in us. And our new birth is also rooted in Christ's resurrection. As Peter puts it, "It is by [God's] great mercy that we have been born again, because God raised Jesus Christ from the dead" (1 Pet 1:3).

Through our new birth, we have become *new creatures* in Christ (2 Cor 5:17; Gal 6:15) and have been given a *new nature* that is set free from the power of sin. So we should "not let sin control the way [we] live," but "give [ourselves] completely to God, for [we] were dead, but now [we] have new life" (Rom 6:12-13).

Having been raised with Christ, we have also been placed in a *new position.* "For he raised us from the dead along with Christ and seated us with him in the heavenly realms because we are united with Christ Jesus" (Eph 2:6). That new position—seated with him in the heavenly places—means we also have a *new focus*: "Since you have been raised to new life with Christ, set your sights on the realities of heaven, where Christ sits in the place of honor at God's right hand. Think about the things of heaven, not the things of earth" (Col 3:1-2). Finally, we have been given a *new passion*: "I want to know Christ and experience the mighty power that raised him from the dead. I want to suffer with him, sharing in his death, so that one way or another, I will experience the resurrection from the dead" (Phil 3:10-11).

Whenever we fail to understand the nature of our life in Christ—that we have been joined to him in his death and resurrection—we always end up viewing the Christian life essentially as an *imitation* of Christ rather than a *participation* in Christ. We turn to the power of the flesh, the power of human self-effort, for enablement and then inevitably look to other sources of spiritual power for provision and protection. Some of the Ephesian believers were tempted to do that. So Paul prayed they would be given a deeper understanding of "the incredible greatness of God's power for us who believe him." That power, he explained, "is the same mighty power that raised Christ from the dead and seated him in the place of honor at God's right hand in the heavenly realms" (Eph 1:19-20). The same identical energy that raised Christ from the dead is thus available to us here and now. Through that "mighty power at work within us," God is able "to accomplish infinitely more than we might ask or think" (Eph 3:20).

How important it is, then, for us to preach Christ's resurrection as something that we share in—not just in the life to come but in our lives today. As Charles Wesley puts it in one of the verses of his great Easter hymn *Christ the Lord Is Risen Today:*

Soar we now where Christ has led, Alleluia!
Following our exalted Head, Alleluia!
Made like him, like him we rise, Alleluia!
Ours the cross, the grave, the skies, Alleluia![15]

Sad to say, many Christians sing those words on Easter Sunday but don't realize what they mean. It is our task as preachers to tell them. Eugene Peterson says it well: "Resurrection gives spiritual formation its energy and character. . . . Jesus' followers live resurrection-formed lives, not by watching him or imitating him or being influenced by him, but by being raised with him. It's formation-by-resurrection."[16]

What good news this is! The Christian life is not essentially *our* life, our human effort at its best for Christ. But *his* life, his resurrection life, being lived through us as we die to ourselves and look to him. Paul sums it up in Galatians 2:20: "My old self has been crucified with Christ. It is no longer I who live, but Christ lives in me. So I live in this earthly body by trusting in the Son of God, who loved me and gave himself for me."

In one of his sermons, Martin Luther said that when we truly grasp and are grasped by this, "that all the works of Christ are done for me, nay they are bestowed upon and given to me, the effect of his resurrection being that I also will arise and live with him, that will cause me to rejoice."[17] Yes, it will! For knowing and living in this resurrection reality, as Paul demonstrates in Romans 6–8, is what sets us free from our bondage to the law and the power that sin has over us. The Holy Spirit that Jesus breathed on the disciples (Jn 20:22) and "the Spirit of God, who raised Jesus from the dead," lives in us (Rom 8:11).

Only this makes our transformation into the image of Christ (Rom 8:29; 2 Cor 3:18) a possibility at all. What hope is there for any of us to put off the old nature and "put on [the] new nature, created to be like God" (Eph 4:24), apart from the presence of his resurrection life in us?

In his unique and inspiring book *Resurrection,* Alister McGrath engages in theological reflection by discussing art and poetry related to Christ's resurrection. At one point he quotes Christina Rosetti's moving poem "A Better Resurrection." A Victorian poet (1830-1894), Rosetti, whose life had more than its share of suffering and trials, poignantly describes here how pointless and futile life would be without the hope of transformation made possible through Christ's resurrection:

> I have no wit, no words no tears;
> My heart within me like a stone
> Is numbed too much for hopes or fears.
> Look right, look left, I dwell alone;
> I lift mine eyes, but dimmed with grief.
> No everlasting hills I see;
> My life is in the falling leaf:
> O Jesus, quicken me.
>
> My life is like a faded leaf,
> My harvest dwindles to a husk;
> Truly my life is void and brief
> And tedious in the barren dusk;
> My life is like a frozen thing,
> No bud nor greenness can I see;

Yet rise it shall—the sap of spring;
O Jesus, rise in me.

My life is like a broken bowl,
A broken bowl that cannot hold
One drop of water for my soul
Or cordial in the searching cold;
Cast in the fire the perished thing;
Melt and remould it, till it be
A royal cup for Him, my King:
O Jesus, drink of me.[18]

Here is a poem written in a dark and somber mood that profoundly speaks of human powerlessness, mortality and decay. In the midst of it, however, Christ's resurrection gives Rosetti cause for hope and rejoicing. Because he is risen—risen indeed—he can rise in us, renewing, transforming and giving us life when we seemingly have no life in ourselves. And so we are enabled to endure and press on, "steadfast, immovable, always abounding in the work of the Lord, knowing that [our] labor is not in vain in the Lord" (1 Cor 15:58 NKJV).

This holds true both in our determination to overcome sin and evil in our own lives and also in our long, seemingly endless struggles to overcome social evils. In the last decade, because of the 2007 bicentennial of the Slave Trade Act (which barred slave trading in the British Empire), as well as a host of new biographies and the release of the film *Amazing Grace,* much attention has been focused on the persevering example of William Wilberforce. In 1787 he recorded in his journal: "God Almighty has set before me two great objects, the suppression of the slave trade and the reformation of manners"[19] (*manners* is a close synonym for morality). Yet the Slave Trade Act wasn't finally passed until twenty years later.

What then enabled Wilberforce to doggedly persist for so long

in the fight against slavery? On February 24, 1791, just a week
before he died, John Wesley wrote a letter to William Wilberforce,
encouraging him, as a member of parliament, in his fight against
slavery. It would be Wesley's last written letter. Here is the first
part of what he wrote:

> Unless the divine power has raised you up to be as *Athana-*
> *sius contra mundum* [Athanasius against the world], I see not
> how you can go through your glorious enterprise in oppos-
> ing that execrable villainy which is the scandal of religion, of
> England, and of human nature. Unless God has raised you
> up for this very thing, you will be worn out by the opposition
> of men and devils. But if God be for you, who can be against
> you? Are all of them together stronger than God? O be not
> weary of well doing! Go on, in the name of God and in the
> power of his might, till even American slavery (the vilest
> that ever saw the sun) shall vanish away before it.[20]

Why, then, was Wilberforce able to persist and persevere? It
must have been, according to Wesley, because God had raised him
up for this task. But before God had raised Wilberforce up, he had
raised his own Son up! And because Wilberforce was a faithful
disciple of his Son, he shared in his resurrection. He could be
raised up because his Lord Jesus had first been raised. As the other
famous Wesley brother, Charles, would have us sing, "Soar we
now where Christ has led."

That's why Wilberforce became not "weary of well doing." He
would have been "worn out by the opposition of men and devils,"
but Wilberforce kept on "in the power of his might." He "soared"
because the same resurrection power that brought Jesus from the
grave dwelled in him, sustained him and strengthened him. That
same resurrection power can dwell in us! Can transform us. Can
give us strength to love and persevere. Have I got a witness? Something tells me that will preach!

LIFE EVERLASTING

The resurrection of Christ not only means spiritual and moral transformation in the present; but in the future, there will also come a day when our earthly physical bodies will be transformed. As Paul tells the Philippians, "He will take our weak mortal bodies and change them into glorious bodies like his own, using the same power with which he will bring everything under his control" (Phil 3:21; cf. 1 Cor 15:53). The resurrected Jesus not only transforms our present. In fact, as Paul emphasizes, "if our hope in Christ is only for this life," we are to be pitied (1 Cor 15:19). Thank God, then, he transforms our future as well.

Through his life, death and resurrection, Jesus has gone before us in defeating and overcoming our last enemy, death (1 Cor 15:26), which came into the world and spread to all creation as a result of Adam's sin. By his victory, Jesus has broken death's power and the power it gave the devil over us (Heb 2:14). Through his triumph, he has set us free from our fear of death and removed its sting (1 Cor 15:56). Many of our classic Easter hymns ("Up from the Grave He Arose," "The Strife Is O'er, the Battle Done") proclaim this theme. None does it better than this verse from Martin Luther's "Christ Jesus Lay in Death's Strong Bands":

> It was a strange and dreadful strife when life and death contended;
> The victory remained with life; the reign of death was ended.
> Stripped of power, no more it reigns, an empty form alone remains;
> Death's sting is lost forever. Alleluia![21]

Contemporary worship songs like Matt Maher's "Christ Is Risen from the Dead" also capture it well:

Christ is risen from the dead
Trampling over death by death
Come awake, come awake
Come and rise up from the grave

Christ is risen from the dead
We are one with Him again
Come awake, come awake
Come and rise up from the grave

O death, where is your sting?
O hell, where is your victory?
O church, come stand in the light
The glory of God has defeated the night.[22]

Of course, any time we preach, there will be those among our hearers who have experienced death as the cruel and relentless destroyer of their deepest hopes and loves. Death came suddenly and snatched away their beloved parent, spouse, child or friend. As a result, they may never have been able to reconcile themselves with life ever since.

Proclaiming the triumph of Easter, then, doesn't mean living in denial about the dark reality of death or skirting around the pain and tragedy of it. Neither does it mean stoically accepting it as an inevitable fate, or viewing it as the eventual conclusion of a natural process. Earlier we referenced what the church father Jerome said, that to understand the antidote you must first understand the poison. Our proclamation of Easter's victory must therefore begin not by denying the reality of death but by staring it in the face and considering what an awful enemy it is. As Rowan Williams puts it, "The resurrection is not properly preached without an awareness of the human world as a place of loss and a place where men and women strive not to be trapped in that loss."[23]

Here then is Fleming Rutledge helping her congregation come to terms with that in an Easter Vigil sermon: "Have you buried someone? If you haven't you will. You will come to know the cold clasp of death. You will know it in the literal sense, when someone who means the world to you is gone, when you yourself must stare it in the face. You will come to know it in a hundred other ways, as the death of a friendship, the death of a career, the loss of youth, the loss of health, the death of happiness, the death of dreams."[24]

In a culture where the subject is often taboo, our preaching needs to confront death for the awful enemy it is and help our hearers grapple with its far-reaching impact on their lives. Jesus himself was no exception. He too faced the reality and crushing finality of it head-on, for he died "a criminal's death on a cross" (Phil 2:8). His amazing miracles and profound teaching, his un-wavering obedience and sublime love for God, all came to a crash-ing halt on Good Friday. He "breathed his last" (Mk 15:37; Lk 23:46). He "tasted death" (Heb 2:9) firsthand. As the Apostles' Creed emphasizes, he was "dead and buried." His life was over and done with. No doubt about it.

In the light of this wretched poison, the terrible tragedy of death, we are then ready to consider the amazing antidote, the astounding triumph of Jesus' resurrection from the dead. Before there was Easter, death imposed an inviolable limit, a final, irre-versible end to human existence. Soul and body were separated. The body decayed, without exception. Period.

But on the third day, on the first Easter, that changed forever. Death itself was defeated. Undone. Its reign came to an end. What was impossible in the sinful, fallen order of things actually happened. In the midst of fallen creation, with its inevitable law of decay and dissolution, of rigor mortis and fixity, *new creation dawned.* "Christ has been raised from the dead," proclaims Paul. "He is the first of a great harvest of all who have died" (1 Cor 15:20). With his resurrection, everything has now changed. As Andrew Purves puts it, "the fundamental structure of human beings has been ineradicably altered from life unto death to life until life through union with him."[25]

According to the New Testament, to bring about this alteration, it was essential and necessary that the resurrection of Jesus was a *bodily* resurrection and not merely a spiritual one. If after his death Jesus had simply morphed into an ethereal, nonbodily form of existence, then, as N. T. Wright explains, "death would not be defeated. It would remain intact; it would merely be redescribed. Jesus, humankind, and the world itself could not look forward to any future within a created and embodied mode such as we now know."[26] In apostolic teaching, resurrection meant the defeat of death, "not simply a nicer description of it."[27]

Jesus' resurrection was therefore, in Gabriel Fackre's words, "no ectoplastic appearance or oblong blur." The resurrection appearances involve an embodied Christ. "Reach out your hand and put it into my side," he says to doubting Thomas (Jn 20:27 NIV). "Touch me and make sure that I am not a ghost," he implores his confused disciples, "because ghosts don't have bodies, as you see that I do" (Lk 24:39). "The bold physicality" found in these appearance stories, notes Fackre, "makes us wince."[28]

In 1 Corinthians 15, Paul is also careful to guard against any notion that Christ's resurrection is simply a prolongation of his former life. His resurrection is not a resuscitation, like a Lazarus returned to an earthly life. Neither has he come back in a purely spiritual, nonbodily mode. Again, we cannot dispense with the body. As J. F. Jansen insists, for Paul and the other New Testament writers, "The risen Christ is some*body* not no*body*."[29]

A few weeks before he died in 1968, the elderly Karl Barth was particularly adamant about this with his former student and friend Thomas Torrance. At one point in the conversation between these two theologians, when the subject of the resurrection of Christ came up, he interrupted Torrance and forcefully declared in German, "Wohlverstanden, liebliche Auferstehung" ("Mark well, bodily resurrection").[30]

We must emphasize and declare it too—despite the militant atheists, skeptical philosophers, and even the theologians and biblical scholars who deny it—the bodily resurrection of Jesus. And the crucial reason we must emphasize it is because the final chapter in the defeat of death—the resurrection of *our* bodies and then the renewal of *all* creation—is absolutely dependent upon it. Because Jesus was raised and given a glorified body on Easter day, a day is coming when "he will take our weak mortal bodies and change them into glorious bodies like his own" (Phil 3:21). All who are in Christ will rise on the day when the risen Christ returns. On that day "when the trumpet sounds, those who have died will be raised to live forever. And we who are living will also be transformed. For our dying bodies must be transformed into bodies that will never die; our mortal bodies must be transformed into immortal bodies" (1 Cor 15:52-53).

When we recite the words of the Apostles' Creed "I believe in the resurrection of the body," this is what we are affirming. And let it be unmistakably clear: what we are envisioning is no mere general affirmation of life beyond death or a Christianized version of the commonly held belief in the immortality of the soul. Again, as Gabriel Fackre insists, this is "no vaporous soul aloft forever in spiritual skies; no passage of a droplet self into an eternal sea; no everlasting memory in the mind of God; no wistful solace based on our influence on generations to come."[31] What we are declaring is the reality of a glorified resurrection body, the new body God wants us to have (1 Cor 15:38).

Then at last, "when our dying bodies have been transformed into bodies that will never die," the Scripture will be finally and fully fulfilled:

Death is swallowed up in victory.
O death, where is your victory?
    O death, where is your sting? (1 Cor 15:54-55)

We wait in eager hope for that day (Rom 8:23) when Christ returns. We also groan with all creation as it "looks forward to the day when it will join God's children in glorious freedom from death and decay" (Rom 8:21). Though we still see death and decay all around us, we remain patient, steadfast and confident. Even in the face of death we can declare, in John Donne's famous words,

> Death, be not proud, though some have called thee
> Mighty and dreadful, for thou art not so. . . .
> One short sleep past, we wake eternally,
> And death shall be no more, Death, thou shalt die.[32]

7

PREACHING
THE ASCENSION

Christ ascended to the right hand of God
that he might lift us up into an ascension life.

A. B. SIMPSON

Closed Thursday for Ascension Day"—the handwritten sign affixed to the front door of Nolt's Bulk Food Store took me completely by surprise. My wife and I and another couple were enjoying a relaxing day trip about fifty miles from our home in the Southern Fork area of Casey County, Kentucky, where a community of more than three hundred Old Order Mennonites have lived since 1976. One of more than twenty Mennonite-owned businesses, Nolt's is known for its canned goods, homemade jams, jellies and breads, fresh spices and herbs, and handmade items like soap and hats. That's why we had stopped at the store, and we certainly weren't disappointed. But who would have guessed anyone here in this rural community in Kentucky would close a store to observe Ascension Day? Most Protestant Christians in North America have never even heard of it.

Commemorating Christ's ascension to heaven, Ascension Day

(also known as the Feast of the Ascension) occurs each year on the Thursday forty days after Easter. Liturgically minded Roman Catholic, Eastern Orthodox and Anglican Christians observe it faithfully. For devout Roman Catholics, it's one of the six holy days of the Christian year where Mass is mandatory. In doing research, I discovered that ever since the Protestant Reformation, Anabaptists such as the Mennonites also have observed and held special worship services on Ascension Day. That's why there was a sign at Nolt's announcing the store would be closed on Thursday.

No doubt, the New Testament writers would be pleased. They believed the ascension of Christ was extremely important and spoke of it often in their preaching. In fact, the Old Testament verse quoted or alluded to in the New Testament more than any other is a verse directly related to it. When I ask pastors and Christian leaders to name that verse, most of them scratch their heads. It's Psalm 110:1: "The LORD says to my Lord: 'Sit at my right hand until I make your enemies a footstool for your feet'" (NIV). According to David M. Hay's scholarly study *Glory at the Right Hand: Psalm 110 in Early Christianity,* that verse is referred to in the New Testament a total of twenty-three times.[1]

However, it's not the Old Testament verse most of us would have chosen, is it? So why do the New Testament writers keep coming back to this particular verse, and why does the ascension play such an important part in New Testament teaching and preaching? Actually, there are two major reasons.

CHRIST'S EXALTED PLACE AT GOD'S RIGHT HAND

First and foremost, the New Testament writers wanted to proclaim something crucially important about Jesus. Not only had he been raised from the dead, but he had also been exalted to God's right hand and enthroned as King. His time of humiliation and death was over, and with the ascension, so too were his resurrection appearances. The ascension therefore signals a decisive transition.

His earthly ministry is complete; his heavenly ministry has begun. As the writer of Hebrews puts it, "When he had cleansed us from our sins, he sat down in the place of honor at the right hand of the majestic God in heaven" (Heb 1:3).

Psalm 110:1 was understood by devout Jews at the time of Christ to refer not only to Israel's past Davidic kings but also to the Messiah who was to come. Convinced Jesus was that Messiah, the early Christians therefore boldly applied it directly to him. After his earthly ministry, they proclaimed, Messiah Jesus, Son of God and risen Lord, ascended and returned to his Lord and Father in heaven, who said to him, "Sit at my right hand until I make all your enemies your footstool."

The New Testament writers therefore keep returning to Psalm 110:1 to proclaim the resurrected Christ's exaltation to the place of honor at God's right hand and his installation and enthronement as King. Paul sums it up, declaring that God's power "raised Christ from the dead and seated him in the place of honor at God's right hand in the heavenly realms. Now he is far above any ruler or authority or power or leader or anything else. . . . God has put all things under the authority of Christ and has made him head over all things for the benefit of the church" (Eph 1:20-22).

Proclaiming the ascension is therefore crucial in fully and properly exalting Christ. For Jesus is not only risen but reigning, not only alive but sovereign, not only central but supreme. As Douglas Farrow demonstrates in his insightful works on the ascension,[2] whenever we fail to proclaim the ascended Christ, enthroned and exalted, something else—our personal agendas, the world's agendas, the church's agendas—moves in to fill the vacuum. Mark it down: when we fail to exalt and enthrone Jesus, something or someone else inevitably assumes the throne.

Raised to New Life in Christ

The early Christians proclaimed the ascension, then, in order to say something crucial about Christ. But they also proclaimed it in order to say something about themselves and the nature of their life in Christ. Having professed faith in Christ and confessed Jesus as Lord, they believed they had been joined to Christ. As Paul repeatedly declared, now they were "in Christ." Therefore the major movements in Christ's life were now movements they were caught up in too.

Paul emphasizes this in Ephesians 2. "We were dead because of our sins" (Eph 2:5), he says, but we have been made alive through faith in Christ. Then he goes on: "He raised us from the dead along with Christ and seated us with him in the heavenly realms because we are united with Christ Jesus" (Eph 2:6). Not only has Christ been exalted and seated at the Father's right hand, but because we are in Christ, Paul says we are there too!

He says the same thing in Colossians 3:1: "Since you have been raised to new life with Christ, set your sights on the realities of heaven, where Christ sits in the place of honor at God's right hand." We have died to this life, Paul insists, and our "real life is hidden with Christ in God" (Col 3:3).

That, then, is the second reason the New Testament writers keep coming back to Psalm 110:1. They believed that not only was Jesus seated on the throne at God's right hand, but since they were now joined to him, they too were destined and invited to sit with him on the throne (cf. Rev 3:21).

Unfortunately, many Christians have little or no awareness of this. Consequently, they never learn to live in Christ from the seated-on-the-throne position that's theirs. No doubt we can be "so heavenly minded we're no earthly good." But if we are going to be any earthly good, according to the New Testament, we must be heavenly minded. That's why focusing on the fact and the significance of Christ's ascension is so essential. As Andrew Murray maintains, "The knowledge of Jesus as having entered heaven for us, and taken us into union with Himself into a heavenly life is what will deliver the Christian from all that is low and feeble, and lift [us] into a life of joy and strength."[3]

In what follows, then, we want to consider the significance of the ascension and how we ought to proclaim it. As in previous chapters, our concern is to focus not primarily on the "what" (the fact and the manner of the ascension) but the "so what" (what implications it has for our personal lives and our congregations).

CHRIST'S ETERNAL HUMANITY

But before we do that, let's remind ourselves that the reason we *can* be united to Christ and seated with him in the heavenly realms is because *he first united himself to us* in becoming flesh of our flesh and bone of our bone. Moreover, that perfect union with our humanity, begun in the incarnation (Jn 1:14), *continues in heaven and throughout eternity.* In *Jesus Ascended,* Gerrit Dawson makes this point well. He quotes Karl Barth, saying that the Son of God maintains our humanity "to all eternity. . . . It is clothing which He does not put off. It is His temple which He does not leave. It is the form which He does not lose."[4]

We need to underscore this because of the incipient gnosticism in much Christian thinking that has tended to spiritualize the ascension. How can earthly, corruptible, decaying human flesh, it is argued, be taken up to heaven? There is no place for it there. So although the eternal Son of God assumed flesh when he became incarnate, when he returned to heaven he must have left it behind. Only spiritual, nonmaterial things are fit for heaven.

Dawson carefully shows, however, how church fathers like Tertullian, Augustine and John Chrysostom consistently stood against such thinking. Tertullian, for example, combated those who he said "excluded from . . . the court of heaven itself, all flesh and blood whatsoever." To the contrary, he boldly declared that "Jesus is still sitting there at the right hand of the Father, man, yet God . . . flesh and blood, yet purer than ours."[5]

In his heavenly existence, he therefore remains fully human. He does not slough off his humanity, but fully retains it. Remember what we emphasized at the end of the last chapter: he has a glorified *body*—yet in a manner appropriate to his heavenly existence. The church fathers realized that if the One who sits at God's right hand is not still fully human (as well as fully God), we will never be able to "enter the veil" and sit there with him.

According to Peter Atkins, the ascension is therefore "the other end of Incarnation doctrine."[6] It means that the incarnation continues, and we are able to enter into the life of God. In fact, this, according to Gerrit Dawson, is "the essential meaning of the ascension." As he explains, "The fully human one has gone within the veil in our name and even in our skin. United to him by the Spirit, to the one who remains united to us, we may follow where he has gone."[7]

But what does it mean to "follow where he has gone"? As we focus now on preaching the ascension, we want to consider that. So let's proceed by asking what the ascension meant for Jesus (where did he go?) in order to discover what it means for us (where do we follow?). "To him who overcomes," says the risen, ascended Christ to the church at Laodicea, "I will give the right to sit with me on my throne, *just as I overcame and sat down with my Father on his throne*" (Rev 3:21 NIV, italics mine). Our invitation to sit with Christ on his throne and Christ's sitting on the Father's throne are bound up together. There is an inseparable connection between the meaning of the ascension for Jesus and its meaning for us, between where he goes and where we follow. So we want to zero in on that.

HOLY-OF-HOLIES PRESENCE

In describing Christ's ascension, Luke says he was "taken up into a cloud" and "rising into heaven" (Acts 1:9-10). The cloud, most scholars agree, is reminiscent of the cloud that descended upon the tabernacle constructed by Moses and the people in the wilderness (Ex 40:34) and the temple built by Solomon (1 Kings 8:10-11). With the cloud came the glory—the Shekinah—the manifest presence of God. "Thus, to enter it," notes Peter Toon, "was to go into the holy of holies, the immediate presence of the Lord."[8]

Heaven, the dwelling place of God in creation, is also closely associated in Scripture with the fullness of the divine presence. Notice how the writer of Hebrews links the two together: "He entered heaven itself, now to appear for us in God's presence" (Heb 9:24 NIV). Heaven, then, is that place that is totally pervaded by God's glory. In fact, according to K. C. Thompson, "What makes heaven Heaven is the immediate and perceptible presence of God."[9]

"He ascended *into heaven*," the creed says. That means Christ has been brought back to the place of the fullness of God's presence. When he became incarnate, the eternal Son voluntarily laid that aside (Phil 2:5-11) and limited himself to an awareness and experience of God's presence through human faculties and consciousness. The ascension means that the period of self-renunciation and self-limitation has come to an end. It means, according to J. G. Davies, that the eternal Son's "consciousness of absolute unity and communion with the Father, which in varying manners and degrees, most notably shown in the cry of dereliction on the Cross, had been limited by the flesh, was fully restored."[10]

The fact that he ascended *into heaven* also means that Jesus is no longer limited by space and time, as he was during his earthly life when he could only be in one place at one time. As N. T. Wright points out, in biblical cosmology, heaven and earth are not two *locations* within the same spatial continuum; rather they are *dimensions* of God's creation. And since heaven relates to earth tangentially, the one who is in heaven can be present everywhere at once on earth. "The ascension therefore means that Jesus is available, accessible, without people having to travel to a particular spot on earth to find him."[11]

Dennis Kinlaw came to that awareness when, as a young pastor, he decided to preach a sermon on the ascension. As he worked on it, he found himself asking two questions: When Jesus ascended, how far did he go? And how long did it take him to get there? As he reflected on them, he broke out in laughter. For he realized "how far?" and "how long?" are space and time questions. And since he created space and time, Christ transcends them and is not bound by them. He is not *in* them, but they are *in* him. As Paul said in his sermon to the Athenians, "He is not far from any one of us. For in him we live and move and exist" (Acts 17:27-28). "Suddenly," said Kinlaw, "I found that I had a sense of his nearness that I had never had before."[12]

He ascended *into heaven*—that's what it meant for Jesus. He has returned to the "place" from which he is able to be present at all times and in all places. What does this mean for those who are in Christ and have been raised up and seated with him in the heavenly realms (Eph 2:6)? It means that while we are here on earth, through the Holy Spirit we're "there" in heaven with him. His prayer "Father, I want these whom you have given me to be with me where I am" (Jn 17:24) is fulfilled in part even now. "Through his grace," Kinlaw came to realize, "God has made it possible for me to live in His presence every moment, so that heaven actually begins for me right now in time and space."[13] Even now while we're "here" we're also "there" with him!

What's more, the ascension means that because Christ is in heaven, he's here—at all times and in all places—on earth with us. When Jesus commissioned his disciples just before he ascended, he told them not to forget that: "And be sure of this: *I am with you always,* even to the end of the age" (Mt 28:20, italics mine). Recognizing and living according to his promised presence is a tremendous spiritual blessing and asset. Jesus is always with us in actual presence. Because we are with him in heaven and he is with us on earth, that means we can live every moment of our lives in the holy of holies presence of God.

When God told Moses it was time to break camp at Mt. Sinai and go up to Canaan, Moses complained, "You have been telling me, 'Take these people up to the Promised Land.' But you haven't told me whom you will send with me" (Ex 33:12). So God gave Moses a wonderful promise: "My Presence will go with you, and I will give you rest" (Ex 33:14 NIV).

Now, however, because Jesus is ascended, that promise is more profoundly true and significant for us than it was for Moses. For he lived under the old covenant, where only once a year the high priest was allowed to enter the holy of holies, the very presence of God. But we live under the new covenant, where Jesus, our great high priest, has opened up a new and living way. Now that we have access to the holy of holies, we can live in the very presence of God every moment of every day.

In "Alleluia, Sing to Jesus," William Dix's wonderful ascension hymn, there is a verse that captures it well:

Alleluia! not as orphans are we left in sorrow now;
Alleluia! He is near us, faith believes, nor questions how;
Though the cloud from sight received him when the forty
    days were o'er
Shall our hearts forget his promise, "I am with you
    evermore"?[14]

To be sure, we may not be consciously aware of God or have a tangible sense of God's presence. But that doesn't change the fact that we are seated in the heavenly realms with Christ and he is always with us. In fact, he's as near to us now as he was to John when the beloved apostle laid his head on his breast during the Last Supper.

So we never have to wonder where Christ is. We don't have to beg him to come on the scene. He is present with us even when he seems most absent. No matter how unholy the situation we may seem to be in, we can be confident he's with us. We are in the holy of holies with him! A. W. Tozer sums it up well: "Ransomed men and women need no longer pause in fear to enter the Holy of Holies. God wills that we should push on into His presence and live our whole life there. This is to be known to us in conscious experience. It is more than a doctrine to be held; it is a life to be enjoyed every moment of every day."[15]

If only we could seize hold of this truth and reality! We are with Christ and Christ is with us. It would transform our lives and our ministries and our congregations. The psalmist declares,

> I have set the LORD always before me.
>   Because he is at my right hand,
>   I will not be shaken.
> Therefore my heart is glad and my tongue rejoices;
>   my body also will rest secure. . . .
>   You will fill me with joy in your presence,
>   with eternal pleasures at your right hand. (Ps 16:8-9, 11 NIV)

We must learn like the psalmist to "set the Lord always before us" and like Brother Lawrence to "practice the presence of God." We must learn to pay attention to God and to pray with St. Patrick, "Christ be with me, Christ within me, Christ behind me, Christ before me, Christ beside me, Christ beneath me, Christ above me." Yet never forget, the ascension of Christ is the sure foundation and the guarantee of this reality. In this event, as Orthodox theologian Patrick Reardon states, "heaven and earth are joined forever."[16] And because God has so joined them together, nothing will ever put them asunder.

RIGHT-HAND-OF-GOD POWER

In helping the Ephesians grasp the power that is at work in them, Paul declares it is the same power that raised Christ from the dead and "seated him in the place of honor at God's right hand in the heavenly realms." The exalted Christ is now "far above any ruler or authority or power or leader or anything else. . . . God has put all things under the authority of Christ" (Eph 1:19-22). As a result of his ascension, Christ has been put in the place of all power, authority and sovereignty.

Again the fact that he ascends *into heaven* signals this. Heaven is the place or sphere from which the universe is sustained and ruled. As N. T. Wright explains, heaven is "the control room for earth; it is the CEO's office, the place from which instructions are given."[17] From here salvation goes forth to the world. Because Christ is in heaven and no longer on earth (located in a particular place and time), he can bring redemption to all places and all times. From there as "the one who ascended," he can "fill the entire universe with himself" (Eph 4:10). No wonder, then, Jesus begins his Great Commission by declaring, "I have been given all authority in heaven and on earth" (Mt 28:18).

The fact that he is now *sitting at the right hand of God* is also significant. As the place of highest honor, it is synonymous throughout Scripture with God's strength, power and authority. For example, in his song of praise and deliverance after God rescued the Israelites by parting the waters of the Red Sea, Moses declares, "Your right hand, O LORD, is glorious in power. Your right hand, O LORD, smashes the enemy" (Ex 15:6). The psalmist extols the greatness of God in a similar fashion: "Powerful is your arm! Strong is your hand! Your right hand is lifted high in glorious strength" (Ps 89:13).

Christ's ascension to God's right hand thus means that he has been given all power and authority. That means the power and authority to carry out the work of redemption and to bring it to full and final consummation have been placed in the hands of the One who sits at God's right hand!

A six-year-old boy and his father were out walking one evening as the sun was going down. The sunset was breathtakingly beautiful, and the young boy had never seen anything like it before. "Wow!" he exclaimed. "Isn't that awesome! God must have painted that with his *left* hand."

His father, puzzled, asked, "Why did you say his *left* hand?"

"Well, at church we say the Apostles' Creed," the boy answered. "And it says that Jesus is sitting *on* his *right* one!"

Not exactly! Jesus isn't sitting *on* the Father's right hand, but *at* the Father's right hand. And because he's seated at the Father's right hand, all power and authority is his. His Father says to him, in the words of Psalm 110:1, "Sit in the place of honor at my right hand *until I humble your enemies, making them a footstool under your feet*" (italics mine; cf. Heb 1:3; 10:12-13).

Of course, many of his enemies refuse to recognize Christ's authority or submit to his rule. So from his position in heaven, seated at God's right hand, he works and watches and waits (cf. Heb 10:12-13) until that day when every knee bows and every tongue confesses that he is Lord (Phil 2:10-11).

He also exercises his power and authority at God's right hand by sending the Holy Spirit and bestowing spiritual gifts on his church so she can fulfill her mission. Although Jesus spoke about the Holy Spirit during his earthly ministry, John the apostle tells us that "the Spirit had not yet been given, because Jesus had not yet *entered into his glory*" (Jn 7:39, italics mine). That would happen only after his death, resurrection and ascension. Then the Spirit would be poured out. And that's exactly what happened on the day of Pentecost (Acts 2:1-4).

Notice too how Peter, in his sermon that day, connects Christ's ascension and the sending of the Spirit: "God raised Jesus from the dead, and we are all witnesses of this. Now he is exalted to the place of highest honor in heaven, at God's right hand. And the Father, as he had promised, gave him the Holy Spirit to pour out upon us, just as you see and hear today" (Acts 2:32-33). Similarly, Paul connects the bestowing of the gifts of the Holy Spirit on the church with Christ's ascension by quoting Psalm 68:18: "When he ascended to the heights, he led a crowd of captives and gave gifts to his people" (Eph 4:8).

"I have been given all authority in heaven and on earth," said Jesus (Mt 28:18). All power and authority to rule until all his enemies are a footstool for his feet. All power and authority to send the Holy Spirit so that the church can fulfill her purpose and mission. That's what the ascension, sitting down at God's right hand, meant for Jesus. Charles Wesley sums it up well in several verses of his magnificent ascension hymn, "Rejoice, the Lord Is King":

> Jesus the Savior reigns,
> The God of truth and love;
> When He had purged our stains,
> He took His seat above.

> His kingdom cannot fail;
> He rules over earth and heav'n.
> The keys of death and hell
> Are to our Jesus giv'n.

> He sits at God's right hand,
> Till all His foes submit,
> And bow to His command,
> And fall beneath His feet.

Each verse of the hymn concludes with a glad refrain: "Lift up your heart, lift up your voice. Rejoice; again I say, Rejoice."[18]

We rejoice too, knowing that when he ascended, he did so not only as God but as the God-Man, the second Adam, the pioneer of a new humanity. That means when we are united to Christ through the Spirit, we can reign with him too! All power and authority has been given to him, and because we are in Christ, we are invited to share in it too. As we have been raised up and seated with him in the heavenly realms, the Father says to us what he says to him: "Sit at my right hand, until I make your enemies a footstool for your feet."

Our "enemies" may include a broad range of things. Difficult circumstances we have to contend with; people who stand against us—some who have hurt us deeply; our own sins, failures and inadequacies; physical and emotional infirmities we struggle with and endure; the world system that hates us because it hates Christ; Satan and all his demonic principalities.

Sometimes we feel overwhelmed by them. Our enemies seem to be making us into a footstool for *their* feet. Because of the ascension, however, and knowing that we are seated with Christ, we can "rule in the midst of [our] enemies" (Ps 110:2 NIV); we can be "more than conquerors" (Rom 8:37). In due time, our enemies will become a footstool for Christ's feet.

The ascension also means that the gift of the Spirit is ours. The ascended Christ baptizes with the Holy Spirit (Mt 3:11; Mk 1:8; Lk 3:16; Jn 1:33). Through the Spirit, both in our personal lives and as communities of faith, we are given power to be witnesses (Acts 1:8), to carry out Christ's mission (Jn 20:21-22), to live victoriously over sin (Rom 8:9; Gal 5:16-25), to overcome weakness (Rom 8:26), to forgive our enemies (Acts 7:55-60), to know we are God's beloved (Rom 1:7; 8:15-16), to be bold and courageous (Acts 4:8-13, 29-31), to use our spiritual gifts (1 Cor 12:4-11), to exercise spiritual authority in Christ (Acts 16:18), to persevere in prayer (Eph 6:18), to patiently endure trials and suffering.

Right-hand-of-God power has been bestowed upon the ascended Christ, and those who are in him share in it too. Paul prays that the Ephesians "will understand the incredible greatness of God's power for us who believe him" (Eph 1:19). Preaching on this aspect of the ascension will help those in our congregations grasp and be grasped by it too.

STANDING-IN-THE-GAP POSTURE

Christ's ascension also inaugurates his work of intercession for us as our great High Priest. The Lord installs him as King, declaring, "Sit in the place of honor at my right hand until I humble your enemies" (Ps 110:1). But he then goes further, declaring the Son has another office: "You are a priest forever in the order of Melchizedek" (Ps 110:4).

Picking up on this priestly dimension of the ascended Christ's work intimated in those words, the writer of Hebrews explains how Jesus was a high priest not simply after the order of Aaron but also of Melchizedek (Heb 7). Unlike Aaron, he became a priest "not by meeting the physical requirement of belonging to the tribe of Levi, but by the power of a life that cannot be destroyed" (Heb 7:16). Because he has been raised and lives forever, his priesthood will last forever. As our eternal high priest, now "he lives forever to intercede with God on [our] behalf" (Heb 7:25). Similarly, Paul declares that Christ Jesus, who was raised to life, "is at the right hand of God and is also interceding for us" (Rom 8:34 NIV).

In fact, according to Thomas Oden, this is "the principal feature of the heavenly session of Christ," that "he enters into an intercessory ministry for humanity in the presence of the Father, pleading humanity's case before the Father."[19] Another Charles Wesley hymn, "Arise, My Soul, Arise," poetically describes this aspect of the work of the ascended Christ:

> He ever lives above, For me to intercede;
> His all redeeming love, His precious blood to plead. . . .
> Five bleeding wounds He bears, Received on Calvary.
> They pour effectual prayers; They strongly speak for me.
> "Forgive him, oh, forgive!" they cry, "Nor let that ransomed
>   sinner die."[20]

So the ascended Christ now engages in a work of intercession on our behalf. He "stands in the gap for us" so that "we have an advocate who pleads our case before the Father" (1 Jn 2:1). Jesus prays without ceasing for his wayward bride, the church. He cries out on behalf of the lost world, the fallen creation he died to save and redeem.

Because our great high priest "understands our weaknesses" (Heb 4:15), his intercession is full of sympathy and compassion. "Made of flesh and blood" (Heb 2:14), fully human like us, he has "gone through suffering and testing" (Heb 2:18) and is able to help us when we are being tried and tested. "It is as our Brother, wearing our humanity," T. F. Torrance reminds us, "that He has ascended presenting Himself eternally before the face of the Father, and presenting us in Himself."[21]

His intercession for us is also intensely personal. Aaron, the Old Testament high priest, wore a chest piece containing twelve gemstones, one for each of Israel's twelve tribes, in order to "carry the names of the tribes . . . over his heart" as he entered into the Lord's presence (Ex 28:29). Likewise, Jesus, our great high priest, holds each of us near and dear to his heart as he presents us to the Father.

If the ascended Christ is now engaged in this high priestly work of intercession on our behalf and on behalf of the world, the fact that we have been raised up and are seated with him (Eph 2:6) means that we too will find ourselves joining him in that work. As we "set our minds on things above" (Col 3:1), we too will be drawn into his work of intercession, assuming a priestly, standing-in-the-gap posture for others.

At daybreak, Jacob tenaciously clung to the angel he had wrestled with all night and cried, "I will not let you go unless you bless me" (Gen 32:26). An intercessor, one who stands in the gap, is like that. Except intercessors don't cry, "I will not let you go until you bless *me*," but, "I will not let you go until you bless *them*"—that family member, or relative, or friend, or congregation, or age group, or people group, or city, or nation, or whatever it is Jesus seems to have laid on their heart. Intercessors stand in the gap for others, pleading to God on their behalf. "Lord, have mercy on them," they implore. "Don't hold it against them. Change their hearts. Cause them to turn to you."

Like Jacob, intercessors are stubborn and persistent, praying, "Lord, I'm not going anywhere. I am digging in my heels. I will stay here until this situation is resolved, until this person comes to you . . . until this congregation is renewed . . . until that church is planted . . . until that people group hears the gospel. Lord, I will not let you go until you bless them."

And make no mistake. Joining with Christ in intercession for others is costly business. In fact, Oswald Chambers maintains that this is the primary way in which we participate in Christ's sufferings.[22] We may find ourselves distraught over some person or situation, agonizing in prayer over it, at times even being led to fast on account of it. As we open ourselves to the Spirit of Christ and identify with others, we are drawn in toward suffering and sacrifice on their behalf. And much to our own amazement—knowing how self-centered we tend to be—we find ourselves joyfully engaging in this form of redemptive suffering.

A few years before his death, Baron Friedrich Von Hugel (1852-1925), the great spiritual director and writer, wrote to his niece about his years of faithful intercession (often in the wee hours of the night) on behalf of one of his daughters:

> I wonder whether you realize a deep, great fact? That souls— all human souls are deeply interconnected? That (I mean) we can, not only pray for each other, but suffer for each other? That these long trying wakings, that I was able to offer them to God and to Christ for my child—that He might ever strengthen, sweeten, steady her in her true, simple, humble love and dependence upon Him? Nothing is more real than this interconnection—this gracious power put by God Himself into the very heart of our infirmities.[23]

Such intercessory prayer grows out of our union with the ascended Christ in his work of intercession. Paul informs the Colossian believers that Epaphras is praying that way for them. "He is always wrestling in prayer for you, that you may stand firm in all the will of God, mature and fully assured" (Col 4:12 NIV). We too are called to such prayer, wrestling on behalf of others.

Sometimes, however, as we find ourselves drawn into that posture, we mistakenly take the burden of intercession on ourselves, as if somehow it depends on us or we have to "make it happen." Then we feel guilty when our passion and fervor subside, and we fail to pray for others the way we know we should. So we need to remind ourselves that our intercession, as significant as it is, is always secondary to Christ's. Remember, he is the principal actor in intercession, not us. As Ambrose insisted, "Unless He intercedes there is no intercourse with God either for us or for all saints."[24] So we are never called to bear the burden of intercession alone, but to be colaborers with him, through the Holy Spirit (Rom 8:26-27), in his ongoing intercession in heaven. When we realize we are called to intercede *with* him rather than *for* him, then we discover that his yoke is easy and his burden is light (Mt 11:29).

Early in her ministry, Amy Carmichael (1867-1951), who spent over fifty years in south India, was given a deep burden for young girls who were dedicated to the Hindu gods and given to temple priests to earn money through prostitution. But as she began to take action in seeking to rescue these temple children, there came a point when the opposition—both human and demonic—became so intense she was ready to give up. Even some of her fellow missionaries stood against her. "You can't 'rock the boat' like this," they warned. "If you keep it up, the government authorities will make us all leave."

As a result, Amy was ready to give up. "Lord," she cried, "this burden you've put on my heart for these girls—I can't carry it anymore." Then one day she realized whose burden it really was:

At last a day came when the burden grew too heavy for me; and then it was as though the tamarind trees about the house were not tamarind, but olive, and under one of these trees our Lord Jesus knelt alone. And I knew that this was His burden, not mine. It was He who was asking me to share it with Him, not I who was asking Him to share it with me. After that there was only one thing to do; who that saw Him kneeling there could turn away and forget. Who could have done anything but go into the garden and kneel down beside Him under the olive trees?[25]

Preaching the ascension—what it meant for Jesus and what it means for us—is to invite Christians to experience, in Paul's words, "every spiritual blessing in the heavenly realms" (Eph 1:3) as they come to know the reality of God's holy-of-holies presence and right-hand-of-God power as never before. But let's be clear, this invitation to an ascension life is not only an invitation to a blessing. It is an invitation to a burden as well—to know and to feel the heart of Jesus for the brokenness and the lostness of others, to go into the garden and kneel down beside him, to assume a standing-in-the-gap posture with him on behalf of others.

"Christ ascended to the right hand of God," says Christian and Missionary Alliance founder A. B. Simpson, "that he might lift us up into an ascension life."[26] What a privilege and a joy for us as we enter into the reality of it! Yet, because preaching the ascension has been so neglected, to paraphrase Paul's words (Rom 10:14), "How shall they know and experience the reality of ascension life if they have never heard about it or been invited into it? And how shall they hear without a preacher?"

8

PREACHING
THE RETURN OF CHRIST

Christ has died . . . Christ is risen . . . Christ will come again.

Once when he was vacationing in Denver, Colorado, President Dwight Eisenhower was reading the local newspaper. His eyes fell on an open letter that told about a six-year-old boy living there named Paul Haley who was dying of incurable cancer. The letter said he had one wish before he died: he wanted to meet the president of the United States.

Spontaneously, in one of those gracious gestures he was known for, Eisenhower decided to grant the boy's request. So on a Sunday morning in August, a big limousine pulled up in front of the Haley home, and out stepped the president. He walked up to the front door and knocked. Dale Haley, the boy's father, in old blue jeans, a faded shirt, unshaven and half-awake, came to the door and opened it. What a shock! There was the president of the United States standing on his doorstep! The chief executive came in, shook hands with Paul, talked to him for a while, took him out to show him the presidential limousine and then left.

In the weeks that followed, the Haleys and their neighbors often talked about what a kind and thoughtful thing Eisenhower did. But there was one person who wasn't entirely happy about it. "Those jeans, the old shirt, the unshaven face," bemoaned Paul's father. "What a way to meet the President of the United States." He regretted that he didn't get up earlier and shave sooner that morning, but because the president showed up unannounced, he was unprepared.[1]

The New Testament speaks often—either directly or indirectly, over three hundred times—about another unexpected arrival. Not of a U.S. president, but of the Alpha and the Omega, the King of Kings and Lord of the whole universe. I'm referring, of course, to the return or second coming of Christ. As he left this earth and ascended into heaven, the angels, who had announced his first coming to the shepherds, told his disciples, "Someday he will return from heaven in the same way you saw him go!" (Acts 1:11). Similarly, the apostle Paul told the Thessalonians, "The Lord himself will come down from heaven with a commanding shout, with the voice of the archangel, and with the trumpet call of God" (1 Thess 4:16).

Yet though Christ's return will be sudden and unexpected—like a thief in the night—it is a return we can prepare for. In fact, many New Testament passages were written with that very purpose: preparing Christ's followers so that, as John says, "when he returns, [we] will be full of courage and not shrink back from him in shame" (1 Jn 2:28).

Later in this chapter we want to consider what Jesus and the apostles tell us about preparing ourselves for his coming. But at this point our concern is more basic and fundamental; namely, how can Christians prepare for something they are largely ignorant and uninformed about?

The often recited Apostles' Creed affirms that "He shall come to judge the living and the dead," and the "Great Thanksgiving" (in the widely used ecumenical liturgy for Holy Communion) proclaims, "Christ has died, Christ is risen, Christ will come again." But in many evangelical and mainline Protestant churches in North America today, the return or second coming of Christ is not exactly a hot preaching topic. In many, apart from the creeds and liturgies and an occasional hymn, it's hardly mentioned at all. The first part of the liturgical season of Advent is partly set aside as a time for contemplating Christ's return. In practice, however, any consideration of his second coming is soon lost in the flurry of Christmas festivities celebrating his first.

CONTEMPORARY VIEWS OF CHRIST'S SECOND COMING

To make sense of the current neglect of North American preaching on the return of Christ, we have to understand our own religious history. Over the past hundred years, American Christians have gravitated toward two extremes on this subject. Ever since the late-nineteenth century when dispensational premillennialism (originally espoused by J. N. Darby earlier in the nineteenth century in England) became the dominant view of the end times among a number of evangelical Christians, a large group of American Christians seem to be obsessed with the second coming and events related to it. According to this end-times scenario, the present world is doomed for destruction, and only a chosen few, who will be snatched up to heaven, will escape. Among this group, speculating about the millennium and the rapture, antichrist and Armageddon, and correlating biblical prophecies with current geopolitical events and nations, never ends. Bestselling books like Hal Lindsey's *The Late Great Planet Earth* and the Left Behind series by Tim LaHaye and Jerry Jenkins continue to fuel a kind of "parousia hysteria," or what N. T. Wright aptly calls "the American obsession with the second coming."[2]

On the other hand, in reaction to this extreme, an opposite group, still suffering from a hangover of twentieth-century mainline liberalism, has so neglected or watered down the meaning of the second coming that it holds almost no significance at all. Here the idea of Christ returning to earth, much like a spaceman, smacks of an outmoded supernaturalism. And his returning to judge conjures up pictures of a wrathful, vengeful deity looking for people to send to hell.

According to this latter view, it's best to demythologize and reinterpret the language of the second coming. Not to be taken literally, it's meant to be symbolic of a time of world renewal when there will be peace on earth for all. Then Jesus will have returned, and his Spirit will rule over all. In his *Outline of Christian Theology* (1901), written during the heyday of American religious liberalism, William Newton Clarke summed it up well: "No visible return of Christ to the earth is to be expected, but rather the long and steady advance of his spiritual Kingdom."[3]

Both of these extremes have contributed to the general neglect of preaching on the second coming in the American church today. Not wanting to be associated with either, many pastors and Christian leaders, while personally affirming the historic orthodox belief in the second coming, simply choose not to preach about it or spell out its implications. Why handle this "hot potato" if you don't have to? Better to leave the subject alone.

Faced with these polar opposites—obsessive "overbelief" on the one hand, and skeptical "underbelief" on the other—how should we preach the return of Christ? How do we chart a third way, offer a third option that challenges both extremes we have to contend with?

On the one hand, we must stand against those obsessed with the second coming and end-time speculation by staying focused on the essentials that all Christians, in all places and at all times, have believed about the return of Christ. It is easy to become preoccupied with nonessential issues concerning the return of Christ about which there has never been consensual agreement in the church. We must insist, then, on keeping "the main thing the main thing" by refusing to be drawn into endless debates over secondary issues or engaging in undue speculation about end-time events.

In Deuteronomy 29:29, there is a helpful distinction between "the secret things" that "belong to the LORD our God," and the "revealed things" that "belong to us and to our children" (NIV). We must hold tightly everything pertaining to the second coming that is clearly revealed in Scripture and has been consensually agreed upon in the church. Those things should be the focus of our teaching and proclamation. But we must hold loosely those secret things concerning Christ's return, which are left unclear in Scripture and undefined by church consensus. We should approach them with a kind of reverent agnosticism, humbly acknowledging we simply don't know and allowing for legitimate diversity over such issues within the body of Christ. Of course, we may speculate about them and have our own opinions, but we must never let them become the focal point of our preaching and teaching. Nor should we allow them to divide us from Christians who hold different opinions. On such nonessentials we must simply agree to disagree in love.

On the other hand, we must also stand firmly against those who downplay the significance of the second coming by equating it with the coming of the Holy Spirit or a future time of peace on earth when the world is finally Christianized. We must insist on the reality of the second coming as an actual happening, an event in the future when the exalted Christ Jesus returns in glory to complete his work of redemption and usher in the grand finale of history.

A watered-down or spiritualized version of the second coming simply will not do. It is contrary to the clear teaching of the New Testament and the consensus of the church. To reject or reduce that clear teaching fundamentally alters the significance of Christ's redemptive work and the message of the gospel. As a result, human redemption (the redemption of our bodies) and the redemption of all creation (new heaven and earth) are forever left unfinished.

Change this part of the Christian story, then, and you have a fundamentally different story. As N. T. Wright insists, the second coming of Christ, rightly understood and interpreted, is "no after-thought to the basic Christian message," nor is it "bolted on to the outside" of a gospel message complete without it. Therefore, "we cannot relegate it to the margins of our thinking, our living, and our praying; if we do, we shall pull everything else out of shape."[4]

We must walk a path between these two extremes, proclaiming the second coming boldly and unapologetically in the light of clear New Testament teaching, yet without becoming obsessed with it or engaging in unhealthy speculation about it. To keep on that path, let me suggest we stay focused on three cardinal truths, three essentials about the second coming that are clearly a part of apostolic faith and the received teaching of the whole church.

THE NATURE OF CHRIST'S RETURN

We must begin by setting forth some basic New Testament teachings about the nature of Christ's return. Because we've neglected to teach and preach on this subject, many in our congregations remain ignorant of these. Even those who seem obsessed with the second coming often get so preoccupied with the events leading up to and following it that they neglect the second coming itself. Here are four essentials about Christ's coming that we need to proclaim.

His return will be personal. The same Lord Jesus—he himself and no other—who lived, died, rose and ascended, will come again (Mt 16:27; Acts 1:11; 1 Thess 4:16). According to N. T. Wright, the main truth, which the early Christians emphasized again and again, "is that *he* will come back to *us*."[5] The one who will be appearing is none other than Jesus, the risen Christ who ascended.

The New Testament writers settled on three main Greek words

to describe Christ's second coming: *epiphaneia* (appearing), *apokalupsis* (unveiling) and *parousia* (coming and presence), which was their favorite (1 Cor 15:23; 1 Thess 2:10; 3:13; 4:15; 5:23; 2 Thess 2:1, 8; Jas 5:7, 8; 1 Pet 1:7, 13; 1 Jn 2:28; 3:2). *Parousia* literally means a person's actual presence, as opposed to absence (1 Cor 16:17; 2 Cor 10:10; Phil 2:12). Outside the New Testament it was often used in a semitechnical way to describe the coming of a king or an emperor to a certain city or nation. Hence it often conveyed the idea of royal presence.

I can remember vividly, as a seventh grader in 1961, when India's first prime minister, Jawaharlal Nehru, came to visit Kodaikanal, the hill station in South India where the missionary boarding school I was attending was located. What a face-lift the town was given in preparation for his arrival! Roads were paved, streets were lighted and litter was removed. All sorts of out-of-the-ordinary things were done because Prime Minister Nehru was coming to Kodaikanal in person. Finally the day came. The athletic field of our school, where he was scheduled to speak, was jammed with people. And there he was! Nehru, the first prime minister of the fledgling nation of India. The local citizens were filled with pride and joy.

We too are getting ready for a personal arrival—that of Jesus, our absent King. He too is coming in person; one day we will see him face to face. And gladness will break like morning when he appears.

His return will be visible. Having disappeared from sight at his ascension, he will reappear at his return. Paul calls it "the *appearing* of our Lord Jesus Christ" (1 Tim 6:14 NIV, italics mine), and John says, "When Christ *appears* . . . we will be like him, for we will see him as he really is" (1 Jn 3:2, italics mine; cf. 1 Jn 2:28). The Greek word John uses here implies the sighting of something that has been out of sight. The same word is used in relation to the first coming of Jesus. Just as Jesus appeared visibly the first time when he became flesh and assumed a human body, he will appear visibly a second time. At present, he is withdrawn and hidden from our view, so we walk by faith and not by sight, but one day when he appears, we shall see him as he is.

His return will be glorious and powerful. As Jesus himself describes it, "And they will see the Son of Man coming on the clouds of heaven with power and great glory. And he will send out his angels with the mighty blast of a trumpet, and they will gather his chosen ones from all over the world" (Mt 24:30-31; cf. Lk 17:24). In his first coming he came in humility and weakness. No one blinked when Mary's baby was born in a stable, and they despised him and turned their faces away (Is 53:3) when he hung on the cross. Not so when he returns. Everyone will take notice. It will be a public, universal, earth-shaking event of biblical proportions.

The New Testament writers use all sorts of dramatic, graphic, cataclysmic and apocalyptic language to drive this point home. Lightning will flash and the skies will light up (Lk 17:24). The trumpet will blast (Mt 24:31; 1 Thess 4:16). The earth will blaze with fire (2 Pet 3:10). The peoples of the earth will wail (Rev 1:7). In interpreting such language and imagery, John Stott wisely suggests that "we must avoid the total literalism which denies . . . any figures of speech at all." Instead we must combine a strong affirmation of a "cosmic event which will include the personal, visible appearing of Jesus Christ" with an "agnosticism about the full reality behind the imagery."[6]

What we can proclaim with certainty is this: though he came as a humble servant, he will return as a triumphant, glorious King. Though he came once to die and make atonement for sin, he will come again "to bring salvation to all who are eagerly waiting for him" (Heb 9:28).

His return is certain to happen, but uncertain as to when it will happen. As sure as we are about the *fact* of Christ's return, we are unsure of its *time*. Here Scripture seems to deliberately leave us with an unresolved tension, what Thomas Oden calls a "purposeful uncertainty."[7]

We find this tension in Jesus' Olivet Discourse, his most extensive teaching concerning his return, found in Matthew 24–25 (cf. Mk 13). His coming, he warns us, will be sudden and unexpected— like a thief in the night. "Two men will be working together in the field; one will be taken, the other left. Two women will be grinding flour at the mill; one will be taken, the other left. So you, too, must keep watch! For you don't know what day your Lord is coming" (Mt 24:40-42). Neither do the angels in heaven, nor even the Son of Man himself know. Only the Father in heaven knows the actual day of his coming (see Mt 24:36). To underscore the sudden and unexpected nature of his return, Jesus then tells the parables of the ten bridesmaids, the three servants, and the sheep and the goats (Mt 25).

However, earlier in his Olivet Discourse Jesus speaks in considerable detail about various signs his followers should look for that will precede his coming: wars and rumors of wars, intense persecution of his followers, the appearance of false prophets, apostasy, the good news preached throughout the world, sacrilege in the temple, natural upheavals and disasters, imminent destruction (Mt 24:3-31). Why then does he describe various signs that his coming is near, but then emphatically insist no one can know when he is coming? Isn't that contradictory?

First of all, we must realize that the various signs of the end that Jesus mentions here (found also in Paul's letters to the Thessalonians and the book of Revelation) are not described so we can calculate the exact time of the end. As George Eldon Ladd maintains, "These events are not signs of an imminent end. . . . Rather than being signs of the end, they are only 'the beginning of woes' (Mk 13:8) *which will mark the entire age.*"[8] These signs, then, will frequently occur *throughout* this present evil age (between the resurrection and the return of Christ) and will only intensify as the actual day of his appearing draws nearer. They will characterize the "beginning of the end," or the "last days" initiated when Christ rose from the dead, but are *not* to be viewed as signs for calculating the precise time of the "end of the end."

The "suddenly strand" and the "sign strand" in Jesus' teaching, as Stephen Travis calls them, are to be looked on as complementary, not contradictory. Thus his teaching about signs of the end "in no way undermines Jesus' rejection of attempts to calculate dates."[9]

Further, we need to emphasize *both* strands and choose to live in the biblical tension of purposeful uncertainty. Without the "suddenly strand" that underscores the imminence of Christ's return, we can too easily get caught up in and focused on the things of this world. We forget that we are citizens of another kingdom and only pilgrims and sojourners here.

However, we also need to emphasize the "signs strand," which causes us to take a long view of history. It reminds us that wars and rumors of wars, false prophets, and natural disasters will occur in every generation, and it guards us against fanaticism, date-setting and shortsightedness. Even as we fervently pray, "*Maranatha,* come, Lord Jesus," as if the day of his coming is "soon and very soon," we should be building and planning for the long-term future, as if that day is not for another thousand years.

Marva Dawn captures this balance well. There are many "signs of the age," she says, such as wars and rumors of wars, earthquakes, and so on. All these "remind us that it is an evil aeon that the reign of God has not come to total fruition." However, these are not the unmistakable "signs of the end" that no one will miss (i.e., when Jesus comes in the clouds). Till then, as Jesus warns, we are "not to go chasing after those who speculate about the end" (see Lk 17:23) but "to be doing kingdom work" such as caring for the needy, telling others of God's love and bringing Christ to bear upon the realities of this world. "We are to remain watchful, to be prepared for the end so that its coming will not take us by surprise, but we are not to chase after it, for no one can know the time of its coming, and its purposes are mysterious."[10]

THE PURPOSE OF HIS COMING
Ironically, many who chase after signs and get caught up with issues related to Christ's return, such as the antichrist, Armageddon, the tribulation, restoration of Israel and the millennium, fail to properly emphasize the purpose of Christ's return. Yet this is what matters most—not *when* he's coming back but *why*—and here the teaching of the New Testament is clear. Keeping this main thing the main thing therefore ought to be the focus of our preaching. We can summarize the purpose of his return under four headings.

Christ will be glorified and acknowledged as Lord and King. We noted earlier that Jesus was revealed as Lord through his resurrection and exalted and enthroned as King through his ascension. In this present age, however, his lordship and reign remain hidden to many. Others stubbornly refuse to recognize it. When he returns, however, that will radically change. Every eye shall see him, and all the nations of the earth will acknowledge him (Rev 1:7). All the kings of the earth will finally "submit to God's royal son" (Ps 2:12). Then at last, Isaiah's prophesy will be completely fulfilled: "The glory of the LORD will be revealed, and all people will see it together" (Is 40:5). That is our blessed hope: the appearing of the glory of our great God and Savior, Jesus Christ (Tit 2:13).

During this present age, the majesty and glory of Christ's lordship is veiled. Hence it can be disputed, misunderstood, scorned and rejected. Those who recognize it and believe in him walk by faith and not sight. As a result, says Walter Kunneth, at the present time the church "bears the 'form of a servant.'"[11]

The parousia, however, is the decisive event when the veil is pulled back and all hiddenness vanishes. The glory and majesty of Christ's resurrection and ascension is made fully manifest. No one will be able to miss it or deny it. All creation—everything and everyone—will bow at his feet. "For it is only when the hidden Lord becomes manifest King in his glory that all resistance to his claim to rule collapses, that indeed every possibility of rebellion has the ground removed from under it."[12]

This includes the resistance and rebellion of Satan and all his evil principalities. Christ won the decisive victory over Satan through his death and resurrection. Yet in this present age Satan has been given permission by God to continue working his evil schemes. When Jesus comes back, however, Satan must go. All Christ's enemies will become a footstool for his feet, and the world will finally say "Good riddance" to the devil. For the first time, the seductive power of the evil one won't have to be reckoned with. Satan and all his demonic powers, which have already been disarmed (Col 2:15), will be subjugated (1 Cor 15:24-25) and destroyed (Rev 20:1-10).

The church of Christ will be glorified and transformed. Christ himself will be glorified when he returns, but he also comes "to be glorified in his holy people and to be marveled at among all those who have believed" (2 Thess 1:10 NIV). Even now, says Paul, we have been raised with Christ (Col 3:1). But "when Christ, who is [our] life, is revealed to the whole world, [we] will share in all his glory" (Col 3:3).

When he returns, then, not only will we see him, beholding him in his glory, but his church will be glorified too. As John Stott explains, "we will be transformed by it and will become vehicles by which it is displayed. . . . We will be radically and permanently changed, being transformed into his likeness. And in our transformation his glory will be seen in us, for we will glow forever with the glory of Christ, as indeed he glowed with the glory of the Father."[13] Just as during his transfiguration, Christ's body became a vehicle for his glory, so when he returns, his body, the church, will become its vehicle as well. Not temporarily, however, as in the case of the transfiguration, but forever and ever. As John the apostle puts it, "When he shall appear, we shall be like him; for we shall see him as he is" (1 Jn 3:2 KJV). And in being made like him, we shall glorify him.

I can never forget a sermon my father, David Seamands, preached based on this text in 1 John, in which he told a personal story to drive home this point. In 1934, when he was twelve years old, Dad's parents, Arnett and Yvonne, returned to India to serve another missionary term. However, for several reasons, they decided to leave David and his older brother, J. T., in the States to live with their maternal grandmother in Wilmore, Kentucky. Little did they dream, though, once back in India, World War II would begin about the time they would be scheduled to return home on furlough.

When the war broke out, it was too dangerous to travel. They were stuck on the other side of the world, and my father didn't get to see his parents for eight long years. Then one day in February when he was a senior at Asbury College in Wilmore, he was attending a class when he received a telegram from his parents that said, "We have arrived safe." It had been sixty-three days since they had left India by freighter, and Dad had not heard from them since. Because of war conditions, they had practically gone around the South Pole before their ship docked in California. They said they were leaving California by train and indicated the time they would arrive at the train depot in Wilmore. It turned out to be exactly on my father's twentieth birthday.

So on a blustery winter morning, he rose early and went down to the depot at 5:00. The train was about an hour late, and as Dad waited, he paced back and forth nervously. He was so excited to see his parents that he was trembling all over. Then finally about dawn the train pulled into the station. His parents were the only ones who got off. Immediately they embraced, but in the haze and gray semidarkness, they couldn't see very well.

Then his mother took his hand, and they walked into the waiting room where it was light. With tears running down her cheeks, she carefully looked her son over from head to toe, and then began to stare at his face. She turned to his father and called him by name. "Arnett, oh, Arnett!" she exclaimed. "He's gone and looked like you! Yes, he's gone and looked just like you."

"In that day when Christ shall appear and we rise with him," my father emphasized as he concluded his sermon, "I believe that at first there will be bursts of praise and celebrations of joy. And then perhaps we'll just worship in silence. But after a while, we'll begin to look in stunned amazement at one another. And suddenly we'll exclaim, 'Why, you look just like *him!* Yes, you look just like him.' For, as John says, 'When he shall appear, we shall be like him; for we shall see him as he is' (1 Jn 3:2)."

"The glory of God is a human being fully alive,"[14] said Irenaeus. So it will be on that day. Christ will come in glory, and his followers will be made fully alive like him. Then Christ will be glorified in his church.

Christ will judge the living and the dead. Although God the Father is spoken of most often as the Judge in Scripture, it is clear from a number of passages that he confers that role on the Son. As Jesus himself acknowledged, "The Father judges no one. Instead, he has given the Son absolute authority to judge . . . because he is the Son of Man" (Jn 5:22, 27). He also declared that when he came in his glory, he would sit on a glorious throne and judge the nations (Mt 25:31-33).

When Peter preached to those gathered in the house of Cornelius, he told them that "Jesus is the one appointed by God to be the judge of all—the living and the dead" (Acts 10:42). Likewise in his sermon on Mars Hill in Athens, Paul declared that God "has set a day for judging the world with justice by the man he has appointed, and he proved to everyone who this is by raising him from the dead" (Acts 17:31). To the Corinthians he wrote that "we must all stand before Christ to be judged" (2 Cor 5:10). And to his son in the gospel, Timothy, he linked Christ's judging of "the living and the dead" specifically with his return, "when he appears to set up his Kingdom" (2 Tim 4:1).

We tend to view judgment almost exclusively in negative terms, as something to be dreaded and feared. And to be sure, there is a negative side to judgment. When he appears, many will shrink from him in fear and shame.

Throughout Scripture, however, judgment is viewed overall in a positive light. As Karl Barth puts it, "In the biblical world of thought, the judge is not primarily the one who rewards some and punishes the others; he is the man who creates order and restores what has been destroyed."[15] When God comes to judge in Scripture, it's not primarily about rewards and punishments or balancing scales, but about fixing what's been broken and making wrong things right.

That's why in many of the Psalms (Ps 7:8; 17:2; 26:1; 35:25; 43:1; 54:1; 119:84), the righteous long and cry out for the Lord to judge. In fact, when the Lord comes to judge the earth, it's an occasion for celebration. The earth is glad and the trees of the forest sing for joy (Ps 96:11-13). N. T. Wright tells us what the judgment celebration is all about: "In a world of systematic injustice, bullying violence, arrogance and oppression, the thought that there might come a day when the wicked are firmly put in their place and the poor and weak are given their due is the best news there can be."[16]

In *The Lion, the Witch and the Wardrobe,* when the White Witch rules Narnia, there is tyranny, cruelty, oppression and death. It's always bleak midwinter and never springtime. Christmas never comes. But there is heartening news that Aslan, the true lord and king of Narnia who will return, is on the move. According to the prophecy,

> Wrong will be right, when Aslan comes in sight,
> At the sound of his roar, sorrows will be no more.

When he bares his teeth, winter meets its death.
And when he shakes his mane, we shall have spring again![17]

So there is great anticipation, excitement and longing for the return of the true king. As Mr. Beaver tells Peter and Susan and Lucy, "Course he isn't safe. But he's good. He's the King I tell you."[18] That's why he comes to make wrongs right. For as Wright insists, "a good God *must* be a God of judgment."[19] Not to ever judge in the face of grave injustices would cast a long, dark shadow on God's goodness.

Preach the second coming, then, as the coming of the Righteous Judge. Let it be an occasion for sober reflection and solemn repentance, but also an occasion of comfort and joy. In the words of Charles Wesley's hymn, "Rejoice, in glorious hope! The Lord our Judge shall come."[20]

Christ will make all things new. As the resurrection of Christ inaugurated the new creation, the parousia, his second coming, will mark its consummation—the new heaven and the new earth (Is 65:17; 66:22; 2 Pet 3:13; Rev 21:1). Even now, Paul tells us, the whole creation is eagerly waiting on tiptoe for that day of great and final transformation (Rom 8:18-25).

According to Paul, "new creation" will unfold in two stages. The first involves the resurrection of our bodies. On that day, "God will reveal who his children really are" (Rom 8:19), he says. Then he elaborates a few verses later: "God will give us our full rights as his adopted children, including the new bodies he has promised us" (Rom 8:23).

As to the nature of our resurrection body, in 1 Corinthians 15:35-53, the apostle speaks in considerable detail. Our bodies will be heavenly and not earthly, spiritual and not physical (in the sense of a *corruptible material* physical body). Yet they will certainly be resurrection *bodies*. We are not destined to become disembodied spirits, but will possess a transformed physicality, or what N. T. Wright likes to call "transphysicality."[21] Paul concludes his discussion by telling us, "It will happen in a moment, in the blink of an eye, when the last trumpet is blown. For when the trumpet sounds, those who have died will be raised to live forever. And we who are living will also be transformed. For our dying bodies must be transformed into bodies that will never die; our mortal bodies must be transformed into immortal bodies" (1 Cor 15:52-53).

Yet what will these transformed, incorruptible, immortal bodies actually be like? Since Scripture doesn't try to provide us with definitive answers, there is little we can say with certainty. But surely C. S. Lewis[22] is on the right track when he imagines they must be more real, solid and substantial than our present ones.

And what will we do with these new bodies? What purpose will they serve? Again, Scripture won't let us say very much, but based on several passages (1 Cor 6:2; 2 Tim 2:12; Rev 5:10; 20:4; 22:5) that speak of God's people reigning, the early Christians believed we will be given new bodies so we will be able to fulfill our original human destiny to rule over the earth. And mind you, it will definitely be a *new* earth, not the one we know now.

This brings us to the second stage in the unfolding of new creation when Christ returns. The one who says, "I am making all things new" (Rev 21:5) meant what he said—*all* things—a new heaven and a new earth, the entire cosmos. No wonder creation is waiting on tiptoe with such great anticipation for that day. For not only shall *we* be made new (the resurrection of our bodies is only the first part of the transformation); but all creation—the heavens, the earth, the entire cosmos—shall also be made new (that's the second part of transformation). God's grand purposes and plan of redemption extend beyond mere human destiny; God will transform and renew everything that he has made.

We cannot begin to fully grasp what that will look like, though John paints some wonderful, inspiring pictures in Revelation

21–22. Peter, however, sums it up well at the end of his second epistle: "We are looking forward to the new heavens and new earth he has promised." And then in the very next phrase, the apostle describes what it will mean: "a world filled with God's righteousness" (2 Pet 3:13).

We can be certain and sure about that; we can hope for that: a world filled with God's righteousness. And given the world today, which often seems filled with so much unrighteousness, how can we not cry, "Come, Lord Jesus. Come back soon"?

PREPARING FOR HIS COMING

According to George Eldon Ladd, Jesus' own teaching about the end times, especially in his Olivet Discourse, is "fundamentally ethical in its character and purpose. He is never interested in the future for its own sake, but speaks of the future because of its impact on the present."[23] The same holds true in the apostles' teaching (1 Thess 5:1-10; Jas 5:7-9; 2 Pet 3:1-14; 1 Jn 3:2-3). Always, and almost effortlessly, they move from eschatology (the day of his coming) to ethics (how then should we live today?).

In his *Psalms of My Life,* Joseph Bayly has a simple prayer that captures it well: "Lord Christ, your servant Martin Luther said he only had two days on his calendar: today and 'that day.' And that's what I want too. And I want to live today for that day."[24] This is what Jesus and the New Testament writers seem most concerned about. They believed that a growing awareness of the certain promise and the approaching nearness of that future day would stimulate, provoke and encourage believers in the living of the present day.

Being watchful concerning that day, looking forward to and longing for it, is essential in strengthening and enabling us "to live today for that day." Anticipating that day actually helps us to live this day, which, in turn, heightens our anticipation of that day. Talk of new heavens and new earth moves us to pray with renewed intensity, "Thy kingdom come on earth as it is in heaven."

Preaching on the second coming should therefore not cause us to abandon this world or look for an escape from its suffering and evil. Instead it should move us to become passionately, actively engaged in it. Let's consider, then, some of the ways the New Testament writers use the promise and anticipation of that day to encourage, provoke and inspire us in the living of these days.

First, our anticipation of Christ's return provokes us to holiness and godliness. Earlier we cited 1 John 3:2 where the apostle declares that when Christ appears, we shall be like him for we shall see him as he is. To be like Christ—that's what we were predestined for (Rom 8:29) and that is our ultimate and future destiny. We are called to be saints, holy ones, conformed to the image of Christ. If that, then, is our future, shouldn't it be evidenced in our active pursuit of holiness of heart and life now? John himself draws out that implication in the very next verse: "And all who have this eager expectation will keep themselves pure, just as he is pure" (1 Jn 3:3).

In fact, throughout the New Testament there is a wide-ranging connection between the second coming and holiness. As David Pawson notes, "The New Testament grounds its appeal for many qualities of sainthood on the fact of Jesus' return. Sobriety, fidelity, moderation, patience, sincerity, obedience, diligence, purity, godliness, brotherly love—all these and more are stimulated by the thought of seeing Jesus again."[25]

Not only does this apply to us as individuals, but also to Christian communities. For the church is destined to be a bride "without a spot or wrinkle or any other blemish . . . holy and without fault" (Eph 5:27). When Christ returns, John envisions a great marriage feast of Christ the bridegroom and his church, the bride (Rev 19:7-9). His bride will have "prepared herself" and been given "the finest of pure white linen to wear," which represents "the good deeds of God's holy people."

If the bridegroom, the church, will be prepared then, shouldn't we as a community of believers be preparing now? That's the force of logic the writer of Hebrews uses to stir and provoke his hearers and readers. "Let us think of ways to motivate one another to acts of love and good works. And let us not neglect our meeting together, as some people do, but encourage one another, *especially now that the day of his return is drawing near*" (Heb 10:24-25, italics mine).

Second, as Jesus indicates in the three parables in his Olivet discourse, his certain return should move us to faithful service. Each of them—the parable of the householder, the ten bridesmaids and the talents (Mt 24:45–25:30), which immediately follow his discussion of the signs of his coming—follow the same plot and make the same point. Someone of power and significance has gone away who is certain to return, though no one knows exactly when. In each parable, there are also those who are wise in preparing for the uncertain time of the return, and those who are foolish and don't prepare.

Those who are "wise," however, are not deemed so because they are able to figure out the exact time the master or the bridegroom will return. Rather, their wisdom is rooted in their faithful, consistent service and actions. As David Pawson observes, "They behaved the same way in the absence of the key figure as they would in his presence. Even a prolonged absence made no difference; they were fully prepared for that. They proved their trustworthiness."[26] Faithful service to the Lord, then, is essential in preparing for his return. And being certain of the promise of that return—not knowing its exact time—is what produces it.

These parables also remind us that faithful service is about persistence and faithfulness, regardless of how significant or insignificant our service appears to be. The master commended the servants who were faithful in little things (Mt 25:21), and the King welcomed the righteous who did things for the least of these (Mt

25:40). Regardless of how significant or insignificant their service, on the day of Christ's return, C. S. Lewis says, "happy are those whom [he] find[s] laboring in their vocations, whether they were merely going out to feed the pigs or laying good plans to deliver humanity a hundred years hence from some great evil. . . . No matter, you were at your post when the inspection came."[27]

Third, anticipation of Christ's return shapes our understanding and engagement in the mission of the church. Our mission, our task, is grounded in the promise of his return and his subsequent renewal of all things. On that day, as we've stressed, the new creation already begun in the resurrection of Christ will be consummated. There will be a new heaven and a new earth. Death and decay, sickness and hunger, slavery and injustice will be no more, and God will fill all creation with his glory and righteousness.

Our mission, then, is to work toward that end. If that's the world's future, we should be doing everything we can, working with God in the power of the Spirit, to get the world ready by moving the world toward it. We should be working to eliminate all the evils that on that day will finally be eliminated and seeking to extend the horizons of God's kingdom on earth as it is in heaven.

Again, this doesn't mean we naively assume we can "bring in the Kingdom" like the old liberal social gospel thought possible. No—new creation will never come out of the old. Jesus himself must return to make all things new. But we can and should engage in work and mission in line with new creation, which moves us "toward the kingdom." That's what the church is called to do, and regardless of the particular shape it takes in light of our particular and varied callings, we can rest assured our work and our efforts in that direction will not be in vain. N. T. Wright sums it up eloquently:

Every act of love, gratitude, and kindness; every work of art or music inspired by the love of God and delight in the beauty of his creation; every minute spent teaching a severely handicapped child to read or to walk; every act of care and nurture, of comfort and support, for one's fellow human beings and for that matter one's fellow nonhuman creations; and of course, every prayer, all Spirit-led teaching, every deed that spreads the gospel, builds up the church, embraces and embodies holiness rather than corruption, and makes the name of Jesus honored in the world—all of this will find its way, through the resurrection power of God, into the new creation that God will one day make. That is the logic of the mission of God. God's recreation of his wonderful world . . . means that what we do in Christ and by the Spirit in the present is not wasted. It will last all the way into God's new world. In fact, it will be enhanced there.[28]

Fourth, anticipating his return encourages us to endure hardship patiently. As James writes to believers undergoing suffering and persecution, "Be patient as you wait for the Lord's return. Consider the farmers who patiently wait for the rains in the fall and in the spring. . . . You, too, must be patient. Take courage, for the coming of the Lord is near" (Jas 5:7-8).

Likewise, in encouraging his readers to wait patiently for Christ's return, Peter reminds them that the Lord is not really being slow about his promise. In his time frame, a day can be a thousand years, and vice versa. Actually, the Lord himself is being patient. In the interim, God is giving people time to repent and time to be saved. We should be patient too as we wait for this to play out (2 Pet 3:3-15).

The connection between the second coming and patient endurance is also particularly emphasized throughout the book of Revelation. John is writing to Christians who are experiencing severe persecution, some of whom will even die for their faith. At the very beginning, he introduces Jesus with a bold, emphatic announcement heralding his return: "Look! He comes with the clouds of heaven" (Rev 1:7). Then John introduces himself: "I, John, am your brother and your partner in suffering and in God's Kingdom and in the patient endurance to which Jesus calls us" (Rev. 1:9). Jesus comes with the clouds of heaven; John is called to patient endurance. The two—Jesus' coming, our patient endurance—are juxtaposed throughout the book. The promise and anticipation of the one gives power and strength for the other.

Finally, anticipating his return fills us with joyful confidence. After all, it's not primarily the end of the world we are waiting for, not even the resurrection of our bodies, but Jesus himself. The second coming is ultimately about a person, not an event. Parousia, we said, has to do with his personal presence. No wonder Paul calls it our blessed hope (Tit 2:13 NIV). Because we know who is coming back, we are full of confidence. There'll be no need to shrink back from him in shame (1 Jn 2:28).

Yes, we rejoice that by faith we know him now, and we experience his personal presence through Word and Spirit and sacrament. But now we know in a glass darkly; then we will know face to face (1 Cor 13:12). On that day our faith shall be made sight and we will know as we are known. If we are rejoicing now, then what a day of rejoicing that will be!

This last point actually helps answer a question my wife, Carol, raised while I was writing this chapter. As I was telling her about it one afternoon, she listened patiently for a while and then said, "Well, if the second coming means all that, then why is it that most Christians today, unlike the early Christians, don't really seem to long for and anticipate the Lord's return? Why do we hardly ever pray like they did, 'Maranatha, come, Lord Jesus' [Rev 22:20]? Eager expectation of Christ's return is a mark of vital New Testament Christianity [Phil 3:20; Tit 2:13; Jude 21]. Why, then, is it so lacking among Christians today?"

Sadly, the absence of our eager expectation of his return is, I believe, the measure of our contentment with the absence of Christ. That's what it finally boils down to. We just don't miss him enough, long to be with him enough, or desire enough that he be with us. And for that we need to repent and pray, imploring Jesus to forgive us and to increase our love-passion for him.

In Christina Rosetti's inspiring poem "After Communion," notice how the wonder and joy of her profound relationship with Christ now moves her to wonder what it will be like then. Notice too how it causes eager expectation and anticipation to rise within her:

> Why should I call Thee Lord, Who art my God?
> Why should I call Thee Friend, Who art my Love?
> Or King, Who art my very Spouse above?
> Or call Thy Sceptre on my heart Thy rod?
> Lo, now Thy banner over me is love,
> All heaven flies open to me at Thy nod:
> For Thou has lit Thy flame in me a clod,
> Made me a nest for dwelling of Thy Dove.
> What wilt Thou call me in our home above
> Who now hast called me friend? How will it be
> When Thou for good wine settest forth the best?
> Now Thou dost bid me come and sup with Thee,
> Now Thou dost make me lean upon Thy breast:
> How will it be with me in time of Love?[29]

Experiencing the risen Christ now, knowing his banner over us is love, being captured by his affection for us, leaning on his breast like John did during the Last Supper—surely, that will cause eager expectation and anticipation to rise within us. It makes us long for more of his presence and stirs up our desire for him to come back. Why? So we can know him more and experience more of his love that surpasses understanding (Eph 3:19).

RENEWING OUR LOVE FOR JESUS

I believe this is the right place to conclude this chapter—and, for that matter, this book. We began by insisting that the North American church needs to recover the Jesus of the New Testament, who is not only central, but supreme in all things. For that to happen, we insisted that pastors and Christian leaders do a better job in communicating the meaning and significance of the work of Christ for our congregations. It's not enough merely to proclaim what Jesus has done. We must also proclaim the so what, that is, what it means for our congregations and personal lives. Hopefully, what we've had to say about his incarnation, death, resurrection, ascension and return will truly help pastors and Christian leaders do that.

But now we finally find ourselves being led to what is perhaps even a deeper problem for us pastors and leaders: our tepid, lukewarm love for Christ, our contentment with his absence in our lives, our lack of a love-passion for Jesus himself. We need to become ardent, wholehearted lovers of Christ—the kind of lovers who set others on fire. For only when our preaching of the significance of what Christ has accomplished for us is coupled with a passionate love in us for Jesus himself, will our congregations be convinced, transformed and renewed.

Our love for Christ, however, is a responsive, not a self-originating, love. We love him, John reminds us, because we have first been grasped by his love for us (1 Jn 4:19). It is the inflow of his love in us that creates an outflow and an overflow of love through us. Let's pray, then, for a fresh encounter with his love that will kindle and renew ours.

"Nothing is more sweet than love," writes Thomas à Kempis in his *The Imitation of Christ*. "The one who loves, flies, runs and is glad . . . is free and not bound." He goes on to describe in considerable detail the amazing, transforming power of love. Then he spontaneously bursts into prayer: "Widen me in love. . . . Let me be possessed by love. . . . Let me sing a song of love, let me follow my beloved on high, let my soul faint in your praise, exalting in love."[30]

Let's make that our prayer too. "Risen Lord Jesus, deepen me and widen me in love for you." May our passionate preaching of what Christ has done for us through his incarnation, death, resurrection, ascension and return be only outdone by our love-passion for the Lord Jesus himself.

NOTES

Chapter 1: Christ Above All

[1]John Calvin, *Institutes of the Christian Religion,* ed. John T. McNeill, trans. Ford Lewis Battles (Philadelphia: Westminster Press, 1960), pp. 527-28.

[2]*The Works of John Wesley,* vol. 1 (Grand Rapids: Zondervan, 1958), p. 103.

[3]Albert Outler, *Theology in the Wesleyan Spirit* (Nashville: Tidings, 1975), pp. 45-46.

[4]Ibid., p. 13.

[5]George Gallup Jr. and George O'Connell, *Who Do Americans Say That I Am?* (Philadelphia: Westminster Press, 1986), p. 119.

[6]Stephen Prothero, *American Jesus* (New York: Farrar, Straus & Giroux, 2003), pp. 11-12.

[7]Richard Fox, *Jesus in America* (San Francisco: HarperCollins, 2004).

[8]On *Morning Joe,* MSNBC, March 14, 2007.

[9]*Talladega Nights: The Ballad of Ricky Bobby,* dir. Adam McCay (Culver City, Calif.: Sony Pictures, 2006).

[10]Prothero, *American Jesus,* p. 297.

[11]Stephen Nichols, *Jesus Made in America* (Downers Grove, Ill.: InterVarsity Press, 2008), p. 10.

[12]David Bryant, *Christ Is All!* (New Providence, N.J.: New Providence Publishers, 2005), p. 15.

[13]Ibid., p. 257.

[14]Michael Frost and Alan Hirsch, *ReJesus: A Wild Messiah for a Missional Church* (Peabody, Mass.: Hendrickson, 2009), p. 92.

[15]Leonard Sweet and Frank Viola, *Jesus Manifesto* (Nashville: Thomas Nelson, 2010), p. xvi.

[16]Ibid., p. 17.

[17]William Willimon, "Preaching in United Methodism Today," *Good News,* January/February 2008, p. 19.

[18]Ibid., p. 20.

[19]Uwe Siemon-Netto, "Barna Poll on U.S. Belief—2001," June 28, 2001, www.adher ents.com/misc/BarnaPoll.html.

[20]Jonathan Edwards, *A Treatise Concerning Religious Affections* (Boston: Kneeland and Green, 1746), part 3, section 12.

[21]Thomas Long, *The Witness of Preaching* (Louisville, Ky.: Westminster John Knox, 2005), p. 13.

[22]Quoted in John R. W. Stott, *The Incomparable Christ* (Downers Grove, Ill.: InterVarsity Press, 2001), p. 161.

[23]Samuel Wolcott, "Christ for the World We Sing," *The United Methodist Hymnal* (Nashville: United Methodist Publishing House, 1989), #568.

[24]William Willimon, *Proclamation and Theology* (Nashville: Abingdon, 2005), p. 3.

[25]Quoted in ibid., p. 17.

[26]Robert Smith Jr., *Doctrine That Dances* (Nashville: B & H, 2008), p. 25.

Chapter 2: Preaching the Incarnation

[1]J. I. Packer, *Knowing God* (London: Hodder and Stoughton, 1973), p. 46.

[2]Athanasius, *The Incarnation of the Word of God,* trans. Penelope Lawson (New York: Macmillan, 1946), pp. 27-28.

[3]Charles Wesley, "Let Earth and Heaven Combine," in *The Wesley Hymnbook,* ed. Franz Hildebrandt (Kansas City, Mo.: Lillenas, 1963), p. 77.

[4]Quoted in Michael Card, *Immanuel: Reflections on the Life of Christ* (Nashville: Thomas Nelson, 1990), p. 31.

[5]Augustine, *Confessions,* trans. R. S. Pine-Coffin (London: Penguin, 1961), p. 145.

[6]E. Stanley Jones, *The Word Became Flesh* (Nashville: Abingdon, 1963), p. 5.

[7]Max Lucado, *God Came Near* (Eugene, Ore.: Multnomah Press, 1987), pp. 25-26.

[8]Ron Newhouse, ed., "Daily Devotions: A Few Moments with God," December 12, 2004, www.devotions.net/devotions/files/2004/12dec/15.htm.

[9]David Bryant, *Christ Is All!* (New Providence, N.J.: New Providence Publishers, 2005), p. 56.

[10]William Blake, "On Another's Sorrow," in *Songs of Innocence.* See www.nimbi.com/songs_of_innocence_on_anothers_sorrow.html.

[11]Dietrich Bonhoeffer, *Letters and Papers from Prison* (New York: Macmillan, 1971), p. 361.

[12]Quoted in Clayton Schmit, "Preaching Is Performance Art," *Christianity Today,* May 23, 2011, www.christianitytoday.com/le/2011/spring/preachingperformance.html.

[13]Quoted in Edward H. Hume, *Doctors Courageous* (New York: Harper & Brothers, 1950), p. 101.

[14]Quoted in Michael Frost and Alan Hirsch, *The Shaping of Things to Come* (Peabody, Mass.: Hendrickson, 2003), p. 64.

[15]Emil Brunner, *The Christian Doctrine of God* (Philadelphia: Westminster Press, 1950), p. 159.

[16]Quoted in William Placher, *Jesus the Savior* (Louisville, Ky.: Westminster John Knox, 2003), p. 17.

[17]Quoted in ibid., p. 21.

[18]Thomas Torrance, *The Mediation of Christ* (Grand Rapids: Eerdmans, 1983), p. 65.

[19]Emil Brunner, *The Divine Imperative* (Philadelphia: Westminster Press, 1948), p. 190.

[20]Jones, *The Word Became Flesh,* p. 30.

[21]Halford E. Luccock, quoted in "Whoops! It's Christmas," in Herbert W. Luthin, *The Abbott Christmas Book* (New York: Doubleday, 1960).

[22]E. Stanley Jones, *The Christ of the Indian Road* (New York: Abingdon, 1925), pp. 191-93.

[23]Frost and Hirsch, *Shaping of Things to Come,* p. 104.

[24]Ibid.

[25]Quoted in Thomas Oden, *The Word of Life* (San Francisco: Harper & Row, 1989), p. 116.

[26]Brunner, *Divine Imperative,* p. 50.

[27]John R. W. Stott, *The Message of 1 Timothy & Titus* (Downers Grove, Ill.: InterVarsity Press, 1996), p. 115.

[28]Bonhoeffer, *Letters and Papers from Prison,* p. 415.

[29]Thomas Merton, *Life and Holiness* (New York: Image Books, 1964), pp. 99-100.

[30]Quoted in Placher, *Jesus the Savior,* p. 46.

[31]Charles Wesley, "Let Earth and Heaven Combine," *The Wesley Hymnbook,* p. 77.

[32]Placher, *Jesus the Savior,* p. 46.

[33]Torrance, *The Mediation of Christ,* p. 75.

[34]Donald Fairbairn, *Life in the Trinity* (Downers Grove, Ill.: InterVarsity Press, 2009), p. 10.

[35]C. S. Lewis, *The Weight of Glory* (Grand Rapids: Eerdmans, 1949), p. 28.

[36]Placher, *Jesus the Savior,* p. 47.

Chapter 3: Preaching the Cross: Scandal, Atonement, Suffering, Love

[1]Quoted in Derek Tidball, *The Message of the Cross* (Downers Grove, Ill.: InterVarsity Press, 2001), p. 20.

[2]Alister McGrath, *The Mystery of the Cross* (Grand Rapids: Zondervan, 1988), p. 19.

[3]Joel Green, "Kaleidoscopic View," in *The Nature of the Atonement: Four Views,* ed. James Beilby and Paul R. Eddy (Downers Grove, Ill.: InterVarsity Press, 2006), p. 166.

[4]Fleming Rutledge, *The Seven Last Words from the Cross* (Grand Rapids: Eerdmans, 2005), p. 4.

[5]Stephen Seamands, *Wounds That Heal* (Downers Grove, Ill.: InterVarsity Press, 2003), p. 48.

[6]McGrath, *Mystery of the Cross,* p. 116.

[7]Alan Lewis, *Between Cross and Resurrection* (Grand Rapids: Eerdmans, 2001), p. 84.

[8]Miroslav Volf, *Free of Charge* (Grand Rapids: Zondervan, 2005), p. 139.

[9]Quoted in Leon Morris, *The Cross in the New Testament* (Grand Rapids: Eerdmans, 1965), p. 410.

[10]George Buttrick, *Jesus Came Preaching* (New York: Charles Scribner's Sons, 1932), p. 207.

[11]Quoted in Morris, *Cross in the New Testament,* p. 411.

[12]Charles Wesley, "And Can It Be That I Should Gain?" *The United Methodist Hymnal* (Nashville: United Methodist Publishing House, 1989), p. 363.

[13]"Were You There," *United Methodist Hymnal,* p. 288.

[14]Frank Lake, *Clinical Theology* (London: Darton, Longman & Todd, 1966), p. 1104.

[15]I deal with this issue in much greater length in my book *Wounds That Heal: Bringing Our Hurts to the Cross* (Downers Grove, Ill.: InterVarsity Press, 2003). Some of the materials in this section and others in this chapter are drawn from it.

[16]Lake, *Clinical Theology,* p. 18.

[17]Ibid, pp. 820-21.

[18]John Stott, *The Cross of Christ* (Downers Grove, Ill.: InterVarsity Press, 2006), pp. 327-28.

[19]Emil Brunner, *The Christian Doctrine of Creation and Redemption* (Philadelphia: Westminster Press, 1952), p. 181.

[20]Quoted in Stott, *Cross of Christ,* p. 310.

[21]Robert Law, *The Tests of Life* (Grand Rapids: Baker, 1968), p. 104.

[22]Quoted in Tidball, *Message of the Cross,* p. 297.

[23]Quoted in ibid., p. 298.

[24]See the introductory chapter in Beilby and Eddy, *The Nature of the Atonement: Four Views,* as well as the chapters written by Joel Green and Bruce Reichenbach, for a helpful discussion of the various issues in the debate.

[25]Michael Gorman, *Cruciformity* (Grand Rapids: Eerdmans, 2001), p. 173.

[26]Isaac Watts, "When I Survey the Wondrous Cross," *United Methodist Hymnal,* p. 298.

Chapter 4: Preaching the Cross: Social Evil, Victory, Dying with Christ
[1]Quoted in Stephen Mott, *Biblical Ethics and Social Change* (New York: Oxford University Press, 1982), p. 12.

[2]Since the mid-twentieth century there has been much scholarly debate about the exact nature of the principalities and powers. See the discussion in John Stott, *The Message of Ephesians* (Downers Grove, Ill.: InterVarsity Press, 1979), pp. 267-75; P. T. O'Brien, "Principalities and Powers, Opponents of the Church," in *Biblical Interpretation and the Church: Text and Context,* ed. D. A. Carson (London: Paternoster, 1984), pp. 110-50.

[3]David Buttrick, *Preaching Jesus Christ* (Philadelphia: Fortress, 1988), pp. 50-51.

[4]Derek Tidball, *The Message of the Cross* (Downers Grove, Ill.: InterVarsity Press, 2001), p. 259.

[5]Paul Fiddes, *Past Event and Present Salvation* (Louisville, Ky.: Westminster John Knox, 1989), p. 200.

[6]Eugene Nida, *God's Word in Man's Language* (New York: Harper & Brothers, 1952), pp. 13-14.

[7]Quoted in Thomas Oden, *The Word of Life* (San Francisco: Harper & Row, 1989), p. 397.

[8]C. S. Lewis, *The Lion, the Witch and the Wardrobe* (New York: Macmillan, 1961), p. 114.

[9]Ibid.

[10]Ibid., p. 133.

[11]John Stott, *The Cross of Christ* (Downers Grove, Ill.: InterVarsity Press, 1986), p. 242.

[12]Ibid., p. 241.

[13]John Taylor, *The Go-Between God* (New York: Oxford University Press, 1979), p. 195.

[14]Tidball, *Message of the Cross,* p. 232.

[15]Michael Gorman, *Cruciformity* (Grand Rapids: Eerdmans, 2001), p. 30.

[16]Dietrich Bonhoeffer, *The Cost of Discipleship* (New York: Touchstone, 1995), p. 45.

[17]Ibid., p. 89.

[18]Charlotte Elliott, "Just as I Am, Without One Plea," *The United Methodist Hymnal* (Nashville: United Methodist Publishing House, 1989), p. 357.

[19]Quoted in Tidball, *Message of the Cross,* p. 238.

[20]Thomas Smail, *Windows on the Cross* (Boston: Cowley, 1996), p. 100.

[21]Tidball, *Message of the Cross,* p. 246.

Chapter 5: Preaching the Resurrection: New Creation, Lordship, Vindication

[1]Luke Timothy Johnson, *Living Jesus* (San Francisco: HarperSanFrancisco, 1999), p. 4.

[2]Ibid., p. 5.

[3]Cited in James H. Charlesworth et al., *Resurrection: The Origin and Future of a Biblical Doctrine* (New York: T & T Clark, 2006), p. 187.

[4]C. S. Lewis, *The Lion, the Witch and the Wardrobe* (New York: Collier, 1986), p. 159.

[5]Ibid.

[6]N. T. Wright, *The Resurrection of the Son of God* (Minneapolis: Fortress, 2003).

[7]In addition to N. T. Wright's work, see William Lane Craig, *Assessing the New Testament Evidence for the Historicity of the Resurrection of Jesus* (Lewiston, N.Y.: Mellen Press, 1989); Stephen Davis, *Risen Indeed* (Grand Rapids: Eerdmans, 1993); Gary Habermas, *The Risen Jesus & Future Hope* (Lanham, Md.: Rowman and Littlefield, 2003); Lee Stroble, *The Case for Easter* (Grand Rapids: Zondervan, 2003); and John Wenham, *Easter Enigma* (Grand Rapids: Baker, 1992).

[8]C. S. Lewis, *Miracles* (New York: HarperCollins, 1974), pp. 236-37.

[9]N. T. Wright, *Surprised by Hope* (New York: HarperCollins, 2008), p. 41.

[10]Ibid.

[11]Ibid.

[12]Neville Clark, *Interpreting the Resurrection* (Philadelphia: Westminster Press, 1967), p. 52.

[13]Wright, *Surprised by Hope,* p. 247.

[14]Ibid., p. 184.

[15]Ibid., p. 46.

[16]David Bryant, *Christ Is All!* (New Providence, N.J.: New Providence Publishers, 2005), p. 15.

[17]Walter Kunneth, *The Theology of the Resurrection*, trans. James Leitch (St. Louis, Mo.: Concordia Press, 1965), p. 131.

[18]Ibid.

[19]Quoted in Richard J. Mouw, *Uncommon Decency* (Downers Grove, Ill.: InterVarsity Press, 1992), pp. 146-47.

[20]Kunneth, *Theology of the Resurrection*, p. 131.

[21]Karl Barth, *Church Dogmatics* 2/2, trans. G. W. Bromiley (Edinburgh: T & T Clark, 1957), p. 248.

[22]Andrew Purves, *The Resurrection of Ministry* (Downers Grove, Ill.: InterVarsity Press, 2010), p. 107.

[23]Quoted in Wright, *Surprised by Hope*, p. 75.

[24]Barth, *Church Dogmatics* 4/1, pp. 310-44.

[25]Jürgen Moltmann, *The Way of Jesus Christ*, trans. Margaret Kohl (San Franscisco: HarperCollins, 1990), p. 224.

[26]John Frederick Jansen, *The Resurrection of Jesus Christ in New Testament Theology* (Philadelphia: Westminster Press, 1980), p. 85.

[27]Quoted in T. F. Torrance, *Space, Time and Resurrection* (Grand Rapids: Eerdmans, 1976), p. 66.

[28]Maltbie Babcock, "This Is My Father's World," *The United Methodist Hymnal* (Nashville: United Methodist Publishing House, 1989), p. 144.

[29]Davis, *Risen Indeed*, p. 201.

Chapter 6: Preaching the Resurrection: Church, Salvation, Life Everlasting

[1]Thomas Oden, *Classic Christianity* (New York: HarperCollins, 2009), p. 710.

[2]D. H. van Daalen, *The Real Resurrection* (London: Collins, 1972), p. 136.

[3]Karl Barth, *The Epistle to the Romans* (London: Oxford University Press, 1933), p. 443.

[4]Van Daalen, *Real Resurrection*, p. 138.

[5]Dietrich Bonhoeffer, *Sanctorum Communio*, Dietrich Bonhoeffer Works, Vol. 1, trans. Reinhard Krauss and Nancy Lukens, ed. Clifford Green (Minneapolis: Fortress, 1998), pp. 14, 198-99.

[6]Dietrich Bonhoeffer, *The Cost of Discipleship* (New York: Touchstone, 1995), p. 241.

[7]Samuel Stone, "The Church's One Foundation," *The United Methodist Hymnal* (Nashville: United Methodist Publishing House, 1989), p. 545.

[8]Thomas Long, *The Witness of Preaching* (Louisville, Ky.: Westminster John Knox, 2005), p. 17.

[9]Quoted in Eugene Peterson, *Living the Resurrection* (Colorado Springs: NavPress, 2006), p. 111.

[10]Stone, *United Methodist Hymnal*, p. 545.

[11]Andrew Purves, *The Resurrection of Ministry* (Downers Grove, Ill.: InterVarsity Press, 2010), p. 44.

[12]Ibid., p. 79.

[13]Quoted in F. B. Meyer, *Our Daily Walk* (Fearn, U.K.: Christian Focus Publications, 1993), reading for March 12.

[14]David Aikman, *Jesus in Beijing* (Washington, D.C.: Regnery, 2003).

[15]Charles Wesley, "Christ the Lord Is Risen Today," *United Methodist Hymnal,* p. 302.

[16]Peterson, *Living the Resurrection,* pp. 107-9.

[17]Quoted in Stephen Davis, Daniel Kendall and Gerald O'Collins, eds., *The Resurrection* (New York: Oxford University Press, 1998), p. 317.

[18]Quoted in Alister McGrath, *Resurrection* (Minneapolis: Fortress, 2008), pp. 57-58.

[19]Quoted in John Stott, *The Incomparable Christ* (Downers Grove, Ill.: InterVarsity Press, 2001), pp 160-61.

[20]Frank Whaling, ed., *John and Charles Wesley* (New York: Paulist, 1978), pp. 170-71.

[21]Martin Luther, "Christ Jesus Lay in Death's Strong Bands," *United Methodist Hymnal,* p. 319.

[22]Matt Maher and Mia Fieldes, "Christ Is Risen," *Alive Again* (Essential Records, 2009). Used by permission.

[23]Rowan Williams, *Resurrection* (Cleveland: Pilgrim Press, 2002), p. 41.

[24]Fleming Rutledge, *The Undoing of Death* (Grand Rapids: Eerdmans, 2002), p. 237.

[25]Purves, *Resurrection of Ministry,* p. 103.

[26]N. T. Wright, *Surprised by Hope* (New York: HarperCollins, 2008), p. 99.

[27]Ibid., p. 62.

[28]Gabriel Fackre, "I Believe in the Resurrection of the Body," *Interpretation* 46 (January 1992): 44.

[29]John F. Jansen, *The Resurrection of Jesus Christ in New Testament Theology* (Philadelphia: Westminster Press, 1980), p. 98.

[30]See Thomas Torrance, *Space, Time and Resurrection* (Grand Rapids: Eerdmans, 1976), p. xi.

[31]Fackre, "I Believe in the Resurrection of the Body," p. 44.

[32]Quoted in McGrath, *Resurrection,* pp. 69-70.

Chapter 7: Preaching the Ascension

[1]David M. Hay, *Glory at the Right Hand: Psalm 110 in Early Christianity* (Nashville: Abingdon, 1973). See for example Mt 22:44; Mk 14:62; 16:19; Lk 22:69; Acts 2:34-35; 7:55; Rom 8:34; Eph 1:20; Col 3:1; Heb 1:3, 13; 8:1; 10:12; 1 Pet 3:22.

[2]Douglas Farrow, *Ascension and Ecclesia* (Edinburgh: T & T Clark, 1999); *Ascension Theology* (London: T & T Clark, 2011).

[3]Andrew Murray, *The Holiest of All* (Tarrytown, N.Y.: Fleming H. Revell, n.d.), p. 65.

[4]Gerrit Dawson, *Jesus Ascended* (London: T & T Clark, 2004), p. 8.

[5]Ibid., p. 32.

[6]Peter Atkins, *Ascension Now* (Collegeville, Minn.: Liturgical Press, 2001), p. 71.

[7]Dawson, *Jesus Ascended,* p. 7.

[8]Peter Toon, *The Ascension of Our Lord* (Nashville: Thomas Nelson, 1984), p. 5.

[9]K. C. Thompson, *Received Up into Glory* (London: Faith Press, 1964), p. 65.

[10]J. G. Davies, *He Ascended into Heaven* (New York: Association Press, 1958), p. 179.

[11]N. T. Wright, *Surprised by Hope* (New York: HarperCollins, 2008), p. 111.

[12]Dennis Kinlaw, *This Day with the Master* (Nappannee, Ind.: Francis Asbury Press, 2002), April 23.

[13]Ibid., March 18.

[14]William Dix, "Alleluia, Sing to Jesus," in *Christian Worship* (London: Paternoster, 1976), p. 208.

[15]A. W. Tozer, *The Pursuit of God* (Camp Hill, Penn.: Christian Publications, 1982), pp. 36-37.

[16]Patrick Reardon, *Christ in the Psalms* (Ben Lomond, Calif.: Conciliar Press, 2000), p. 91.

[17]Wright, *Surprised by Hope*, p. 111.

[18]Charles Wesley, "Rejoice, the Lord Is King," in *The Wesley Hymnbook*, ed. Franz Hildebrand (Kansas City, Mo.: Lillenas, 1963), p. 97.

[19]Thomas Oden, *Classic Christianity* (New York: HarperCollins, 2009), pp. 488-89.

[20]Charles Wesley, "Arise, My Soul, Arise," in *Wesley Hymnbook*, p. 84.

[21]Quoted in Dawson, *Jesus Ascended*, p. 133.

[22]Oswald Chambers, *My Utmost for His Highest* (Westwood, N.J.: Barbour, 1963), p. 258.

[23]Douglas Steere, ed., *Spiritual Counsel and Letters of Baron Friedrich von Hugel* (New York: Harper & Row, 1961), p. 78.

[24]Quoted in Richard Foster, *Prayer: Finding the Heart's True Home* (New York: Harper-Collins, 1992), p. 193.

[25]Amy Carmichael, *The Gold Cord* (New York: Macmillan, 1932), p. 31.

[26]A. B. Simpson, *The Christ of the Forty Days* (Camp Hill, Penn.: Christian Publications, 1995), pp. 144-45.

Chapter 8: Preaching the Return of Christ

[1]Billy Graham recounts this incident in *World Aflame* (New York: Doubleday, 1965), p. 207.

[2]N. T. Wright, *Surprised by Hope* (New York: HarperCollins, 2008), p. 119.

[3]William Newton Clarke, *An Outline of Christian Theology* (New York: Scribner, 1901), p. 444.

[4]Wright, *Surprised by Hope*, p. 142.

[5]Ibid., p. 124.

[6]John Stott, *The Message of 1 and 2 Thessalonians* (Downers Grove, Ill.: InterVarsity Press, 1991), pp. 105-6.

[7]Thomas Oden, *Classic Christianity* (New York: HarperCollins, 2009), p. 798.

[8]George E. Ladd, *The Presence of the Future* (Grand Rapids: Eerdmans, 1974), pp. 326-27.

[9]Stephen Travis, *I Believe in the Second Coming of Jesus* (Grand Rapids: Eerdmans, 1982), p. 93.

[10]Marva Dawn, *In Our Weakness* (Grand Rapids: Eerdmans, 2002), p. 36.

[11]Walter Kunneth, *The Theology of the Resurrection* (St. Louis, Mo.: Concordia, 1965), p. 278.

[12]Ibid.

[13]Stott, *1 and 2 Thessalonians*, pp. 149-50.

[14]Quoted in Nonna Harrison, *God's Many-Splendored Image* (Grand Rapids: Baker Academic, 2010), p. 50.

[15]Karl Barth, *Dogmatics in Outline* (London: SCM Press, 1949), pp. 134-35.

[16]Wright, *Surprised by Hope*, p. 137.

[17]C. S. Lewis, *The Lion, the Witch and the Wardrobe* (New York: Collier, 1986), pp. 74-75.

[18]Ibid., p. 76.

[19]Wright, *Surprised by Hope*, p. 137.

[20]Charles Wesley, "Rejoice, the Lord Is King," *The United Methodist Hymnal* (Nashville: United Methodist Publishing House, 1989), p. 716.

[21]Wright, *Surprised by Hope*, p. 44.

[22]See especially his imaginative presentation in C. S. Lewis, *The Great Divorce* (New York: Macmillan, 1946).

[23]Ladd, *Presence of the Future*, p. 327.

[24]Joseph Bayly, *Psalms of My Life* (Wheaton, Ill.: Tyndale House, 1969), p. 42.

[25]David Pawson, *When Jesus Returns* (London: Hodder & Stoughton, 2003), p. 69.

[26]Ibid., p. 65.

[27]C. S. Lewis, "The Christian Hope," *Eternity* 5 (March 1954), p. 50, quoted in Travis, *I Believe in the Second Coming*, p. 123.

[28]Wright, *Surprised by Hope*, pp. 208-9.

[29]Christina Rosetti, "After Communion," in *The Complete Poems of Christina Rosetti*, vol. 1, ed. R. W. Crump (Baton Rouge: Louisiana State University Press, 1979), pp. 228-29.

[30]Thomas à Kempis, *The Imitation of Christ*, trans. E. M. Blaiklock (London: Hodder & Stoughton, 1979), pp. 97-98.